THE DOLLAR

THE DOLLAR

Sir George Watson Lectures

1953

BY

ROY HARROD

F.

NEW YORK

HARCOURT, BRACE AND COMPANY

first American edition

LIBRARY OF CONGRESS CATALOG CARD NUMBER: 54-6383

PRINTED IN THE UNITED STATES OF AMERICA

PREFACE

When I was honoured by an invitation to deliver the George Watson lectures on American history, literature and institutions, it at once occurred to me that I was not a deep scholar in this field and that, if I accepted, I was in danger of lowering the high standard that has been maintained. My affection for America, however, made the invitation tempting, and, on reflection, it occurred to me that the dollar might properly be regarded as an American 'institution'. Indeed it must be so regarded. It is an institution with a complex history, deeply interwoven with the whole story of the great American adventure. On this thought, I at once began to look at the matter more affirmatively. As early as 1926, I had advertised a course of eight lectures in the University of Oxford on the Federal Reserve System, somewhat to the surprise of my colleagues. Once every two years until the Second World War broke out, I gave eight lectures under the same title, but naturally the contents changed greatly.

The treatment of the dollar that I here present has had to be selective. I have stressed what strike me as the key episodes. It has been a pleasure to me to go over the old story again, and it is my hope that I shall succeed in conveying some of this pleasure even to readers who are not economists and will have to take some of my reasonings on trust. Currency history is full of surprises. It deals with matters that are at the same time close to and far removed from the everyday thinking of ordinary people; a decision has to be taken by an administrator of no recondite knowledge or great theoretical grasp; for instance, the Indian mint is closed to silver; this is reported in the newspapers and its proximate meaning and consequence may be understood by those affected and by the general public; but its true significance and lasting consequences are veiled; mysteries of great moment masquerade as humdrum routine matters. If this is true of the past, it is no less so of the current events among which we live; their true purport constantly eludes us. The layman may console himself with the thought that the economist is often as little able as he to interpret contemporary happenings; it is only the economic historian who can perceive the pattern in retrospect. To study the past may at least make us wary, give us some inkling of what is likely to be important now and heighten our interest in what is proceeding around us.

In the later part of this book, I have set out my ideas about what we have come to know as the dollar problem of to-day. This can be analysed by looking at the list of things that we need to buy from the United States and asking whether we really need them. Or we may attempt a more profound analysis of the international disequilibrium, using fine tools of economic theory. We shall do still better, if we can bring in the time dimension and interpret the present behaviour of the dollar at least in part in terms of the characteristics with which its history has endowed it.

R. H.

September 1953

CONTENTS

THE DOLLAR

I

EVOLUTION OF THE DOLLAR

SIR GEORGE WATSON endowed these lectures to com-
memorate the tour of the Prince of Wales, now Duke
of Windsor, in the United States. Subsequent events
could not detract from the value of the work he did
then nor reduce its claim to commemoration, and I am
particularly happy to be the person appointed to remind
you of it this year. I am convinced that when future
historians have to describe how it happened that the
sad events connected with his abdication did not in the
least impair the position of the Crown in the Commonwealth and Empire, they will attribute it far more to
King Edward's clear perception that it was his duty
somehow to secure precisely that result, than to the
efforts of those with whom he had to negotiate. Other
members of his family, forebears and successors, have
displayed high kingly qualities in the discharge of their
normal functions; it fell to him to exercise those same
qualities in arranging for his own withdrawal from
them; that was perhaps the hardest task of all; and in
its discharge the kingly qualities shone most brightly.

The lectures are arranged by the Sulgrave Manor
Board. We English have long since learned to venerate
the great George Washington; the wisdom and dignity
of his bearing towards the English when he was President contrasted with much pettiness that was still displayed on this side; from him, I believe, lessons can
still be learnt by those in both countries on how a mag-
nanimous spirit can assuage differences. There were
some Englishmen indeed who retained their admiration

for Washington even while the War of Independence was still proceeding. This comes quite near home to me. My landlord and dear friend, Commander Roger Coke, is directly descended from Coke of Norfolk, who voted against the American War, and proposed and carried by one vote a motion in the House of Commons to recognize American independence in February 1782. 'Every night during the American War', he told a sheep-shearing party at Holkham long afterwards, 'did I drink the health of General Washington as the greatest man on earth.'[1]

Having spoken of Washington, I cannot forbear mentioning an episode that recently came to my attention, since it has its piquancy on this occasion. Among the forebears of Mr. Adlai Stevenson was one Joshua Fry, who according to most American historians had his education at my university.[2] Later professor of mathematics at William and Mary College, county surveyor, justice of the county, justice in the court of chancery, county lieutenant, first cartographer, along with Jefferson's father, of Virginia, he was given command of a detachment in 1754 which had to proceed through the valleys and capture Fort Duquesne (Pittsburgh) from the French. During the expedition, he fell from his horse and was killed. His second-in-command took over. This was George Washington, and it was in the successful completion of that campaign that he made his reputation as a soldier. But what if Fry had not fallen?

It is time for me to focus your attention upon the dollar. To some, the dollar may appear no more than a symbol, 'the dollar sign', or a method of calculation, involving a tiresome process of conversion, of no greater

---

[1] Quoted from 'A Report of the Transactions at the Holkham Sheep-shearing, 1821', by R. N. Bacon, in *Coke of Norfolk and his Friends*, by A. M. W. Stirling, vol. i, p. 190.

[2] They identify him with the Joshua Fry who matriculated at Wadham on March 31, 1718. See Foster's *Alumni Oxonienses*.

interest than when one needs to convert bushels into tons. Rightly understood, every great currency has a vitality and character and, one may say, a personality of its own. If one wants to consider problems of the balance of payments of a currency, one will not get far unless one has a good conception of this personality. The personality may be due to characteristics of the nation concerned; it may also reflect the personalities of great men (or women) who have had in the past a decisive influence in shaping the currency.

If I may digress for a few minutes upon another great currency more familiar to most of us here, I would say that one should not be able to fix one's thoughts on the pound sterling without getting a whiff of the personalities who were responsible for its essential historic characteristics — Queen Elizabeth I, Thomas Mun, Isaac Newton the astronomer, David Ricardo and Walter Bagehot. The refusal of Queen Elizabeth I to countenance debasement constitutes the main watershed, not only in the history of British currency, but also, by precedent, in the history of the currency of Christendom since the Dark Ages. It was owing to the firm insistence of the virgin queen, that a secret plan for collecting in all the bad old coins with great rapidity was successfully executed — a remarkable achievement for those days. This striking *coup* demonstrated the importance that was to be attached to sound discipline in currency matters. It was due to Mun's influence that the doctrine was established and afterwards maintained that if a nation wanted to have a prosperous foreign trade and an abundance of good money in internal circulation, it was necessary to allow absolutely free export of the precious metals. Paradoxical at the time, this doctrine also came to have recognition far beyond England. Newton, the astronomer, brought to the currency question not so much those gifts that made him the father of modern physics as that insatiable appetite for particular detail that he displayed in the study of biblical chronology. Delving into the curious lore of gold and silver parities, degrees of fineness, mint charges and the like, he established the gold and silver values of British currency after a long period of considerable disorder and confusion, and his gold rating of the pound sterling showed its merit by surviving unaltered until 1931. Ricardo laid down the principles of convertibility and the quantity theory of money. A Member of Parliament during the period when sterling remained inconvertible after the Revolutionary and Napoleonic Wars were over, he pooh-poohed the idea that it was necessary to build up large reserves before restoring convertibility, and indeed recommended the sale of gold from the reserve as a better method of achieving that goal. Bagehot established the doctrine, not without many years of polemics as leader writer on the *Economist* newspaper, that in a crisis it was the duty of the Bank of England to lend to all and sundry who could offer security, if necessary far beyond what might seem the limits of prudence and the Bank's own resources. The triumph of Bagehot's views relieved England of the series of crises which had previously plagued her. In these varied contributions to the philosophy of sterling, there was something paradoxical when they were first propounded. Together they gave sterling its essential character during its period of greatest ascendancy. More recently sterling has had a troubled and indeed hectic history, and some of its old characteristics are in abeyance; but it continues to show vitality in spite of being subject to vast pressures, and this may be in part due to the survival of that faith in it which was fostered by the characteristics aforementioned.

It is a matter of regret that one cannot readily think of any great name to link with sterling since Bagehot. In the case of the dollar, there is happily one such in more recent times. The character of the dollar to-day owes much to that great man, Benjamin Strong, Governor of the Federal Reserve Bank of New York from the outset until 1927.

The dollar has had a tumultuous history. Sterling, except in the most recent period, had been very staid and stolid by comparison. The dollar has indeed reflected the characteristics of the American nation, its incredible achievements in the last century and a half, its bursting energy, its conquest of space, its vast progress in production and transportation. At times the dollar has been swept along by great waves of American economic expansion. There have been tremendous proliferations of banks and paper issues with consequent bouts of inflation. A cautious student, ignorant of the future, observing only the phenomenon of some great expansive and inflationary period, might well have been inclined to pronounce the dollar doomed. Yet the extraordinary thing is that, despite these phases, it has stood its ground and, anyhow up to 1933, retained its gold value almost at the level prescribed by Alexander Hamilton. The expansionist, enthusiastic, exuberant Americans met the stern, unbending Americans, and the result was compromise, by which the currency was rescued from the whirlpools and preserved intact for future use.

Learned historians of the dollar are apt to find their sympathies lying naturally with the stern, unbending Americans, and it is not to be denied that in saving the dollar from destruction they played a vital part. But I find the historians a little one-sided, and neglectful of the fact that the exuberant, enthusiastic Americans may have also played a complementary part. It is possible that from time to time those expansions of paper issues, to which the strait-laced school so much objected, assisted the Americans in straddling a vast continent in quick time, and establishing world supremacy in production.

Now that the dollar has become an institution of international significance, Americans concerned with such matters have to cast their eyes around the world. It is the stern, unbending Americans who are the experts and professionals in these matters, and it is with their thinking that the outside world is likely to be confronted. The exuberant, expansionist Americans are not, for the most part, monetary experts; they have been concerned to get on with their all-absorbing jobs and determined to burst the bonds of excessive monetary puritanism. They played their essential part in creating the American that we know. If we, who live outside the dollar area, find ourselves occasionally chafing at the dogmatism of the stern, unbending Americans, we may reflect that we are doing no more than the majority of Americans themselves have done from time to time to the advantage of their own country. Perhaps we should take a leaf out of their book.

It may seem unsound to speak in this way at a time when insufficiently curbed inflation in various parts of the world has been doing great harm. For a number of years since the war, the stern, unbending attitude of the Americans has been a salutary influence. But the situation is rapidly changing, and thinking should be related to the future, not less than to the past. Too narrow a strait-jacket, corresponding to the thinking of the stern, unbending Americans, may impede progress. I give one example of what I have in mind. I have always been, and remain, a strong advocate of sterling convertibility, and I believe that the lack of sufficient disinflationary policies during the quinquennium following the Second World War has been injurious to the British economy. But in the changed circumstances of to-day, any further turn of the screw of disinflation, even if it could be proved that that was both necessary and sufficient for restoring the dollar convertibility of sterling, would be a fatal error.

I propose to give you some of the elementary facts of the history of the dollar. It is important that you should think of it not simply in terms of the U.S. trade balance of yesterday, but in the round, with the time dimension added. I confess to the hope that before I conclude these lectures, I shall have succeeded in setting out the causes of what we have come to know recently as the 'dollar problem'. But that cannot be to-day.

The first question that may occur to us is why the United States has a dollar. This first comes into history at an official level when the Continental Congress on June 22, 1775, declared that the two million bills of credit which they were issuing to finance the war for freedom should be redeemable in Spanish milled dollars.[1] Why not in pounds or shillings? It may occur to you to suppose that this action was a deliberate thrust at the oppressor country, a form of ideological, or shall we say terminological, warfare. But I do not think that this interpretation is a true one. The real cause was more practical.

This was basically the fissiparous tendency in the colonies prior to the war. There had been a number of paper issues and sundry currency irregularities which from time to time evoked reproof, but not decisive reforming measures, from London. The consequence was that there were many different kinds of shillings in the colonies, the New England shilling, the New York shilling, the Pennsylvania shilling, each with quite different values in terms of the English shilling. It was these differentiated colonial shillings that were in actual circulation, whereas the foreign currencies, many of which were moving around, were naturally uniform throughout the colonies. Should the Continental Congress tell Pennsylvanians that its bills of credit were redeemable, not in Pennsylvanian shillings, but in New England shillings? It could not make them redeemable

[1] *Journals of the Continental Congress from 1774 to 1788*, vol. i, p. 87.

in one or other alternatively, since these various shillings had quite different values. Among the foreign currencies in circulation, the Spanish milled dollar, which came in by trade across the frontier of Louisiana, happened to be about the best; so this was chosen. These dollars, and thereby one may say the United States dollars of to-day, are none other than the coins known in romantic literature as pieces of eight. It is perhaps germane to the question of ideological warfare to observe that Hamilton records as late as 1791 that all accountancy was still carried on in terms of English pounds, shillings and pence.

The next step was taken in July 1785, when the Continental Congress declared the dollar the official money and established a decimal system. This, however, was merely a declaration and nothing was actually done at that time.

It fell to Alexander Hamilton, that man of great genius, to establish a mint in 1791. He addressed himself to the problem with his wonted thoroughness. First he had to consider whether the United States should be monometallic or bimetallic. I shall have more to say in the course of what follows about the bimetallic question, since the history of the dollar in the nineteenth century is much connected with this. I suppose that there are many persons now alive whom reference to the bimetallic controversy no longer thrills. I am not one of them. It is roughly true to say that highbrows incline to bimetallism, while the naïve and simpleminded favour monometallism. Hamilton, for all his being a man of action and decision, of great driving power and of fierce passion, was essentially a highbrow — can anyone who reads his works deny it? Accordingly he opted for bimetallism. And that was accepted.

It is interesting to observe that in his classic State Paper, the only man whom he mentioned by name was Isaac Newton, and he based his decision for a 15:1

ratio of silver to gold on Newton's authority.[1] He admitted that time had passed since Newton's verdict, but did not think the forces great enough to overset it.[2] Hamilton's gold valuation of the dollar survived, subject unfortunately to a minor change in 1834, till 1933. It is pleasant to think, as we can if we waive the small change in 1834, that the gold valuations of those two great currencies, sterling and the dollar, as they remained until about twenty years ago, both stemmed from the brain of the famous astronomer. It is also pleasant to think that the dollar valuation came via the endorsement of Alexander Hamilton, that master mind and great ornament of his country.

So far, all seems fair. But it has unfortunately to be admitted that these dollars of Hamilton's, gold and silver, did not come into active circulation for many decades. They were for the time being mere pipe dreams, or, if I may mix my metaphors in relation to coins, they were on paper only. Let us consider the silver dollar first. The trouble was that at this time foreign coins were also admitted to the status of legal tender. To have displaced them by native coins would have entailed a vast administrative effort, and there was much else to be done in the United States in 1791, so that Hamilton may be excused for not pressing the matter further. The United States mint, as established, produced some admirable silver dollars, whose craftsmanship is very fine and worthy of the highest American standards. But just for this reason these coins, when they entered into competition with the mass of miserable foreign coinage that was circulating, immediately fled the country under Gresham's Law. Gradually a

---

[1] He quotes Newton as giving a spread from 14·5 : 1 to 15 : 1; as the movement since Newton's time has been on the whole favourable to gold, he was right to choose the higher ratio.

[2] Alexander Hamilton, *Works,* ed. by Henry Cabot Lodge, vol. iv, p. 21.

regular circuit was developed. The U.S. coins were shipped away, while dud coins came in and had to be accepted by the U.S. authorities in legal discharge of debt. The U.S. government was involved in sheer loss on the expenses of minting. Eventually this matter became a scandal, and in 1806 it was felt that something must be done. By then Hamilton had not only passed from the administration, but had met his tragic death. Thomas Jefferson was a great architect, a great constitutionalist and a great American; but to the best of my knowledge he did not win spurs as a currency expert. His recipe was to stop minting silver dollars. If one finds the coinage system in great disorder, one may think it appropriate to stop wasting one's time minting coins; that is certainly a Draconian solution and appeals to common sense: but perhaps it is a little negative; it does not seem to have a very constructive character. Wise after the event, we may say that what ought to have been done at this time was not to close, but to enlarge, the operations of the mint, and at the same time to declare all the foreign coinage legal tender no longer, compensating the existing holders. This would have been a difficult administrative task, requiring the Elizabethan touch. The consequence of Jefferson's solution was that the coinage remained very bad for a number of decades thereafter.

Hamilton's gold dollar raises more interesting issues. He established the ratio at 15:1. In his State Paper he made no reference to Calonne's ratio of $15\frac{1}{2}:1$, which was established in 1785 and took the place of the previous French ratio of about $14\frac{1}{2}:1$; the change was probably designed by that financier to secure a capital gain to the government, with which to buttress the tottering finances of the *ancien régime*. Reference to it in 1791 might be deemed unnecessary, since the French economy was then inundated by inconvertible assignats and the ratio was inoperative. It is more probable that Hamilton just overlooked it. Napoleon, a stalwart metallist, managed to re-establish convertibility despite his war-mongering, and the Calonne ratio came into operation in 1803.

Golden dollars were not minted in the following years, and this may well have been due to the fact that the supplies of paper dollars were quite sufficient. In his *Considerations on the Currency and Banking System* (1831), Albert Gallatin attributes the dearth of gold in the United States to the French ratio of $15\frac{1}{2}$: 1 being more favourable to gold than Hamilton's ratio of 15 : 1.[1] It is difficult to judge of this through the mists of time; it is not quite evident, having regard to transportation costs, mint charges and delays, that the French ratio was divergent enough to exert a decisive pull. Gallatin observes in the course of his argument that gold only began to be drawn out of the United States in 1821, and he attributes this to causes connected with the balance of trade. Such causes are not a wholly satisfactory explanation, since, if the French ratio was really pulling, silver could be sent in exchange for gold, whatever the balance of trade. Gallatin refers to the year 1821 as a mere date, such as any other might have been, and makes no specific comment on it. But to the English reader it leaps to the eye; for 1821 was the year in which England returned to the gold standard, after a period of inconvertible paper lasting twenty-four years. English commerce was probably more important in the general picture at this time than French commerce. The fact that the drain started in 1821, suggests that the pull was really due to the restoration of the gold standard in England and not to the divergence of the French ratio.

But even if the French ratio was in fact pulling gold out, that cannot be accepted as a sufficient reason for

[1] *The Writings of Albert Gallatin.* Edited by Henry Adams, vol. iii, p. 304.

altering Hamilton's ratio, as was done in 1834, when 16 : 1 was substituted for it. It is essential to the bimetallic system that one should take very long views, tolerating periods in which one or other metal becomes unavailable; it will not work in any other way. There was no real need for gold coins in the United States at that particular period, since there was plenty of paper to satisfy the need for large denominations. More generally, a bimetallic nation, temporarily losing gold, can always replace it by large denomination silver certificates; alternatively, if it loses silver, it can replace that by token coins. That is how the bimetallic system works smoothly. It is undermined by chopping and changing to meet temporary situations.

On the whole, it was probably unfortunate that Hamilton's ratio was altered. Had it been maintained, the Californian discoveries would, as it happened, have supplied the United States with plenty of gold afterwards, so that there was not much gain on that side. What is more important is that if Hamilton's ratio had continued in existence, the American system would have been more receptive to silver from the mines of Nevada, and that might have made a big difference to the currency history of the whole world. On balance, I judge it a pity that Hamilton's ratio was changed at that time.

The reason alleged by Gallatin and other writers for the desire to make a change was the discovery of gold deposits in North Carolina and Georgia. If these authorities are right, but I do not pronounce upon them, it can be said that Congress raised the dollar price of gold by 7 per cent. to provide a home market for domestic output.

The matter was not done without consideration. Ingham wrote a State Paper and Gallatin an essay, from which I have quoted. There were successive reports from a Congressional Committee, and the matter was amply discussed. The names I have hitherto mentioned have been names well remembered and rightly honoured in American history. I do not know if the name of C. P. White of New York echoes down the corridors of time; it does not resound in my ears; if this was an American of distinguished service, I must apologize for my lack of recognition. He was chairman of a committee which produced two reports in favour of a ratio of 15·625 : 1, and expert opinion seemed to converge upon this ratio as correct. But when the matter came for final debate in 1834, White made a dramatic tergiversation and declared for 16 : 1. Other speakers warned Congress that this would mean giving up all hope of ever having silver dollars coined; and these predictions proved correct. But despite much learned reasoning, Congress seem to have acted in the spirit of making a day of it, and voted for 16 : 1. Silver dollars, which had hitherto been kept out of circulation by the foreign currencies, were kept out of circulation thereafter by that Act.

Before leaving this Congressional discussion, I must refer to another American, Mr. Gorham, whose name does not echo down the corridors either, but ought to. In the great bimetallic discussions in England, Alfred Marshall put a suggestion before a Royal Commission, for a scheme known as symmetallism, which is commonly referred to in text-books. His idea was that instead of a promise to pay being legally dischargeable by a certain weight of silver, or by a certain weight of gold, or by a certain weight of silver *or* a certain weight of gold alternatively, it should be dischargeable by the tender of a certain weight of gold *and* a certain weight of silver taken together. Of course this would not necessarily involve the handing over of the two actual metals; the actual medium could be either, or token coins or paper, the system being kept in being by the willingness of the central bank to buy and sell and by arbitrage. It was an ingenious device to obtain certain alleged advantages of bimetallism while avoiding the inconveniences. The British Commission, writing in terms of politeness due to the venerable professor, rejected the proposal as not likely to win public support. It has continued, however, to be mentioned as being thought to carry the germ of a much larger idea, namely that of a currency that shall have a stable value in terms of commodities generally. If a debt has to be discharged by means of so much gold *and* so much silver, why not by so much gold and so much silver and so much copper, etc. etc.— in fact by the whole basketful of commodities in terms of which it is desired to maintain the currency stable ? The great Marshall has been credited with the authorship of the idea of symmetallism.

But more than fifty years earlier, Mr. Gorham put it forward to the House of Representatives on June 21, 1834.[1] The terms of his amendment are worth quoting :

Be it further enacted that from and after the first day of January 1840 the legal tender for the payment and discharge of all debts contracted or obligations for the payment of money incurred after the passage of this act, shall be one-half in silver coins and one-half in gold coins which by law shall be made current in the United States.

Congressmen rejected the proposal on much the same grounds that Marshall's proposal was rejected half a century later, but with less courtesy than was displayed to the professor. I do not know if Mr. Gorham was cherished by his family and honoured by his State as a wisehead. He has not achieved a place in the *Dictionary of American Biography*. Therefore it is well that we should let our minds dwell for a moment with piety across the century upon a man who has not received due credit.

[1] *Abridgement of the Debates of Congress, 1729–1856.* Edited by T. H. Benton. New York, 1860 (Appleton & Co.), vol. xii, p. 511.

The silver coinage remained in a shocking and disreputable condition for a number of years more. Gallatin made an unfavourable comment in 1831 on the English token coinage of silver as recently established.[1] He held that it would lead to a sort of multiple currency system in which small obligations would be discharged in a debased currency on different terms from larger obligations. His aspersion has been criticized as not corresponding to the facts, as indeed it did not. The English token silver coins had for some time been circulating at par in an orderly way. None the less, it is instructive to notice that Gallatin's criticism was a valid inference from the existing legislation. In 1798 the English mint was closed to silver, as a temporary measure during the period of inconvertibility. The Act of 1816, which defined what the position of silver was to be when cash payments should be resumed, provided for a substantial seigniorage charge on silver coins but authorized the reopening of the mint to unlimited silver coinage. In the event, on the resumption of cash payments in 1821, this provision was never put into effect. Had the law been carried out, Gallatin's criticism would no doubt have been verified by experience.[2] There is a striking parallel between the abandonment by Britain and the abandonment by the United States of the silver part of their systems. Both did it when their actual circulating medium consisted of inconvertible paper, the British in 1816 by means that would have been ineffective if carried into effect, the Americans, not quite by accident but with insufficient forethought, in 1873. In such ways do far-reaching monetary changes occur.

In 1853 Congress authorized an issue of silver tokens from one-half a dollar downwards, having limited legal

[1] *Op. cit.* p. 310.
[2] Cf. the observations on this episode by Professor R. G. Hawtrey, *Currency and Credit*, 1st ed., p. 302; 3rd ed., p. 349.

tender. And so it happened that, after a lapse of more than sixty years, the United States at last came to enjoy a silver coinage of her own. It is to be noted, however, that Hamilton's full value silver dollar remained on the statute book. It could not come into circulation at that time because of the 16 : 1 ratio (1834). None the less its existence *in posse*, paradoxical though this may seem, was one of the great bulwarks of the bimetallic world.

In February 1873 it was abolished. This was an Act of momentous import. Later that year the countries of the Latin Union, of which France was the most important member, closed their mints to silver, and thus brought to an end the world-wide bimetallic system, which had lasted for some five centuries; its demise had far-reaching effects on the monetary equilibrium in all countries.

Historians of recent date are apt to pass over the American Act of 1873 as a thing of trivial significance. Even that most learned historian, my friend and former colleague, Professor Samuel E. Morison, mentions it only in a footnote, and refers to it as an act to convert ambiguities of coinage.[1] This was by no means the way in which it was regarded by many distinguished Americans a few years later, who habitually referred to it as the 'crime of 1873'. I have sympathy with that expression.

When gold monometallism became a kind of orthodoxy, there was a tendency to decry the arguments of the other side as spurious and special pleading. There are many notable examples in currency history of a rather strong tendency to close the subject when once a certain step has been taken. There seems to be something peculiar to the nature of currency that makes it especially painful to reopen questions. Historians, such as A. B. Hepburn, have made the most of the point that

[1] *History of the United States*, vol. ii, p. 384.

some of the bimetallists who inveighed against 'the crime of 1873' themselves partook in the legislation, which was thoroughly discussed, and made no demur. What right had they therefore to refer to a crime, when they had themselves been as responsible as others for it? This is a good debating point, but at a deeper level it may lack justice. What happened was perfectly understandable.

When the Act was passed, it seemed doubly removed from being likely to have any influence. In the first place, greenbacks were still inconvertible, and remained so until 1879, and consequently the American bimetallic par at that time was altogether inoperative. Secondly, Hamilton's silver dollar had never been in circulation. How, one might ask, could it possibly make any difference to anything to abolish a coin that had been on the statute book for eighty-two years but had never in fact been used? Complacency about the possible effects of the abolition of the coin in February 1873 was certainly understandable, and, one may say, forgivable. None the less it was wrong. The Act may have been subjectively innocent and yet objectively a crime, and hence the apparent inconsistency of the persons in question. One must consider their state of mind.

If a certain number of countries have a bimetallic system, that makes the whole world bimetallic, since it establishes a fixed ratio between the metals in the markets of the world. Bimetallism may be said to have come into existence within the century after the coining of gold florins in Florence in 1272. It subsisted for five centuries. During that time gold rose against silver very gently, from about 11 : 1 to about 16 : 1. This is clearly a very gradual movement when spread over five hundred years. But once the bimetallic par was finally ruptured in the autumn of 1873, silver fell to 19 : 1 within seven years and to 35 : 1 before the close of the century. The magnitude of the change is evident. The relative constancy of the ratio had lasted so long that it would be beyond the imagination of any normal person to suppose such a complete reversal possible. Some people fall into thinking that something which has been going on no more than five years belongs to the order of nature. How much more natural must it be to take something that has been going on for five hundred years for granted? The bimetallic par had existed for many generations before Columbus set sail. Who would think that something so well embedded in the established order of things could be changed by Congress taking a non-existent coin off the statute book?

It only remains to consider how far 'the crime of 1873' did in fact alter the course of events. There was a paradox also in what was happening on the other side of the Atlantic. During the 'sixties, the inflow of gold from California and Australia and its exclusion from the American circulation by inconvertible greenbacks were putting the bimetallic countries of Europe under pressure. Gold came into these in great abundance and their silver coins were fast disappearing. At length, in 1865, they clubbed together in what was known as the Latin Union, to provide for a uniform token silver coinage that would supply a medium of small change to take the place of the disappearing full value silver coins. How untimely! If only they could have tided over another year or two, silver would have come flowing in from Nevada and their difficulties would have been at an end. Just as the existence of the American tokens made it easy to get rid of the Hamilton silver dollar in February 1873 without too much fuss, so the Latin Union tokens facilitated the still more fateful closing of their mints to the five-franc piece in the following September. Currency historians, especially those who wrote before 1914, are apt to write currency history as a triumphal progress from primitive barter to the glories of a fully fledged gold standard. An alternative way of regarding it is as a tantalizing succession of missed opportunities.

The Latin Union countries which had been oppressed by the abundance of gold in 1865 came under the opposite pressure only eight years later. They were flooded with silver from Nevada, and gold was being drained away. Of this the most important cause was the decision by those, whom Karl Marx unkindly called the 'mushroom upstarts' of the new German Empire, to transfer from silver to gold monometallism. England was taken to be the foremost economic power, and she had prospered on gold monometallism. It seemed to be the smart thing to do to follow her example. Reasoning of this kind has some merit, but also demerit. Whether the maintenance of the Hamilton silver dollar would have caused the bimetallic countries to pause before this final abandonment of silver must remain in doubt. But there is a much more important point to make in this connection. The United States returned to specie payments in 1879. But had the Hamilton silver dollar remained on the statute book, silver would have begun to flow into the American circulation as soon as the discount on silver against gold in the world markets became as great as the discount on greenbacks against gold. It seems that this would have happened some time in 1876. Silver would then have flowed into the American circulation and have sunk no further in world markets. What would have happened then? I am aware that historical hypotheses are often looked upon with severe disfavour. As I am not a professional historian, I will proceed without qualm. I am convinced that currency history is full of lessons and that an understanding of history can be of value in influencing judgement and decision about current matters. How can one assess the importance and merit of a given act, if one is debarred from speculating about what would have happened, had it not occurred?

In the circumstances I have envisaged, the United States would have been holding the silver baby, and would have demanded international conferences to elicit support from other powers in sharing the burden. Even as things turned out, she called for and obtained three such conferences, in 1878, 1881 and 1892. Her final effort was made when she despatched three commissioners to Europe in 1897, consisting of Edward Oliver Wolcote, Charles J. Paine and Adlai Stevenson (grandfather). The silver advocates of the United States found much support for their point of view, not only from the former bimetallic countries in Europe, but from Britain also. Although by this time inured to gold monometallism herself, Britain was deeply concerned about the Indian rupee, which was deteriorating rapidly in the world's markets. No doubt much nonsense was talked about the evils due to the fall of the rupee, but it cannot be denied that some of the evils alleged were real. Moreover, England herself was suffering from deflation and depression, and this was attributed to the breakdown of world bimetallism. Gold had now to do much of the work in the world that silver had done before, and there was just not enough gold to go round ; a long period of falling gold prices occurred.

None the less the conferences achieved nothing, despite the lively and keen desire in many quarters that something should be done to restore silver. The reasons of this failure can be fairly summarized under three heads : (1) The rot had gone so far that it was too late to do anything. How familiar this point of view, when it is a question of repairing a mistake ! (2) No one country was strong enough to restore a par and sustain bimetallism for the world by her unaided action. (3) There was not enough momentum in international co-operation at that time to secure agreement about all the complicated matters involved, including presumably the choice of a new parity. Again how familiar it all sounds !

But how totally different the position would have been at these conferences if the Hamilton silver dollar had not been abolished in 1873. The world would have had a rude shock when the par was ruptured in 1873 — assuming, that is, that the Latin Union had, none the less, closed their mints — and then, two or three years later, the United States would have come to the rescue, to the joy and relief of all, as her silver dollars flowed into circulation. The silver rot would not have gone so far, and the other nations could not have argued that it was too late for them to co-operate. There would have been a demonstration that one nation could temporarily at least hold the par. And how much easier international co-operation would have been in those circumstances; indeed not much co-operation would have been called for; all that would have been needed would have been for the Latin Union countries to restore a parity, convenient to themselves and to the Americans, probably equal to the *de facto* ratio at the time, based on the content of the Hamilton silver dollar and the current gold value of the greenbacks.

However, the 'crime' was committed and all turned out otherwise. There arose in the United States a violent agitation on behalf of silver; it can probably be said that at no period of history has a currency question played such an important part in the politics of a nation. The tide of agitation grew ever stronger and higher and was symbolized in the classic expression 'mankind's crucifixion upon a cross of gold'. One must keep one's sense of proportion, for in this period, the last quarter of the nineteenth century, the United States was making gigantic strides in production and trade, her exports were rapidly mounting and she established a world leadership in the productivity of her industry. If this was a crucifixion, what would have been a state of health and freedom? Although one must not exaggerate, one should recognize that the evils complained of were real. The progress of the country was interspersed with crises of great severity, and it may be that these interruptions were more severe and entailed more loss and suffering than they would have, had not the narrowness of gold base been engendering deflation. It is arguable that Britain, where interest in the silver question hardly amounted to an agitation, suffered more, although the view is also held that the deflationary pressures of those days spurred producers to more efficient methods.

Agitation in the United States mounted ever higher as the years wore on, until one fine day a *deus ex machina* appeared in the form of a mighty stream of output of gold from South Africa, which flowed round the world and bore gold in large quantities to the United States. The application of the cyanide process to the South African deposits killed the bimetallist agitation in the United States and everywhere else. The narrowness of the gold supply was to cause trouble again, notably in the 'twenties; but by that time bimetallism had been forgotten, and men looked in other directions for recipes. The United States owed much to the advent of South African gold. For the last time I will venture a historical hypothetical. It is surely safe to say that if this South African gold had not appeared, Bryan, who so nearly achieved success in the presidential election of 1896, would have become President of the United States in 1900. And then the fun would have begun.

Meanwhile attempts had been made to support silver in subsidiary ways. The Bland-Allison Act of 1878 provided for the purchase of silver in greater quantities than were needed for the token silver coinage, and silver certificates of large denominations were issued. This helped silver somewhat, but did not have the potent effect of a parity. The Sherman Law (1890), which still further enlarged the purchases, was repealed in 1893. By this year the decline of silver had proceeded so far that Britain felt it needful to take India off the silver standard, which had the natural consequence of a further depression of silver. In 1900 a consolidating Act was passed confirming gold monometallism in the United States.

To bring the narrative up to date it remains only to mention the Roosevelt devaluations of 1933, but these were so closely connected with the circumstances of the world slump that I must defer discussion of them.

We must now retrace our steps. I have given an outline of the metallic standard. But, in the United States, paper has always played a foremost part in the actual circulation. This is in line with the progressiveness of the United States, for paper belongs essentially to a more advanced phase in monetary development than full-weight coins.

We have seen that the Continental Congress began issuing bills of credit in 1775. This was a principal method of financing the war. As can easily be imagined, issue succeeded issue to sustain the historic struggle, rampant inflation occurred, and by 1781 the public for the most part did not even bother to take up the offer of one new paper dollar for a hundred of the old. The issues of the Continental Congress just petered out. Hamilton, severe disciplinarian that he was, has argued that the issues were justified; the Continental Congress had no regular system of taxation at its disposal, and the supreme urgency of the struggle for freedom justified the expedient of inflation.[1]

When war is over, the citizen hopes for a return to normalcy. But then tiresome problems of reconstruction arise. And these may entail new inflationary pressures. In the Confederate period, these problems became very acute. One may think of the dollar that we know as having been created by the United States. But one may also think of the matter the other way round, and argue

[1] Alexander Hamilton, *Works*, vol. iii, pp. 320 and ff.

that it was the dollar problem that created the United States.

Capital was required for reconstruction, but was not easy to come by. In most states the governments made advances for purposes of reconstruction in the form of paper notes, and the danger of renewed inflation appeared. Coercive measures were sometimes attempted. It was the farmers then, as at some other periods, who wanted easy money, to enable them to make good the ravages or neglect of wartime. The mercantile community was on the other side. They had to make payments to foreigners and wanted something better than depreciated paper notes. The most crucial conflict between the two interests was in Massachusetts, where the mercantile element was strong and succeeded in defeating an inflationary measure in the legislature in 1786. But the farmers were not content to take this reverse lying down, and Shay's rebellion broke out and had to be put down by force. Thus only five years after the struggle for liberty, blood was shed in fratricidal conflict. For a number of years, thinking men had realized that a stronger form of federal government was needed to cope with commercial policy, tariffs, revenue and, above all, to give the country a uniform and stable currency and avoid renewed inflations. Shay's rebellion brought this thinking to a head.

When Washington, acting with sage discretion, convened a conference at Annapolis to arrange co-operation among the states concerned with the waters of the Potomac, we may be sure that he had these more momentous and controversial issues in which co-operation was also required at the back of his mind. More states were invited than were concerned with the Potomac, and, although the attendance was disappointing, it was sufficient to give birth to the greater conference at Philadelphia. Once assembled, the thoughtful leaders of the country could devote themselves with gusto to the much more congenial and, shall we say, more glamorous task of constitution making. But it was the economic confusions and, notably, the problems connected with the indiscriminate issue of dollar bills by states and the spotlight on this problem provided by Shay's rebellion that gave the actuating force in bringing the conference together. It is interesting in this connection to observe that Rhode Island, where the farmers won a victory for paper money in the state legislature at about the same time that those of Massachusetts were defeated, was the last of the original states to join the Union.

The state issue of paper money was squarely prohibited in the constitution. As regards a possible federal issue, nothing was said either way. Hamilton, who in other matters was always prepared to interpret the implied federal powers latent in the constitution liberally, affirms [1] that 'the spirit of that prohibition [of state issues] ought not to be disregarded by the Government of the United States . . . the wisdom of the government will be shown in never trusting itself with the use of so seducing and dangerous an experiment'. There was doubt about the constitutionality of the greenbacks issued during the Civil War. But war is exceptional. The question of the right of the federal government to issue notes in peace-time was eventually decided in a favourable sense in the case of Juillard *v.* Greenman in 1884. While it is no doubt necessary to bow to the opinion of the Supreme Court on the legal issue, Alexander Hamilton's authority is so great that his clear dictum on the question of expediency will continue to be remembered.

It is to Hamilton that we look for the next stage in this history. When still a soldier in the War of Independence, he wrote a memorandum (1780) [2] on the

---

[1] Alexander Hamilton, *Works*, vol. iii, p. 413.
[2] *Ibid.* vol. iii, p. 319.

need for what we now call a central bank to Robert Morris, also a revered name, who was then struggling against gigantic difficulties to provide finance for the Continental Government and may be said to have rescued it from financial ruin, but later passed into a debtors' prison on his private account. Hamilton's reasoned statement is a truly remarkable document for a man of twenty-three. It is the more so in that it is written only four years after the appearance of Adam Smith's *Wealth of Nations*, and some thirty years before Ricardo began his series of classic contributions. Hamilton has often been praised for his precocity; he was indeed precocious in a double sense, both for bothering his head when so young about such matters, and for outlining a scheme essential for his country, which was not, however, destined to be permanently established there for another 130 years.

The memorandum was interesting but not without faults, and by no means of the high quality of his great State Paper of 1791, which was a masterly exposition of the subject. He accordingly founded the Bank of the United States, which operated as a central bank, but with an interruption of six years, until 1836. It can hardly be doubted that it played a decisive part in the establishment of a relatively sound financial structure during this formative period.

It was, however, never popular. There were always doubts about its constitutionality. Hamilton persuaded Washington that it was covered by the implied powers in the constitution. Up-country it was feared that it was a vehicle of foreign influence. It had an aroma that was uncongenial, being connected in men's minds with the esoteric finances of the old world, and seemingly divorced from the tasks of the free and individualistic citizens of the new Republic, who were nearer to primitive reality, conquering the soil, laying the physical foundations of a great economy. It was connected, too, with the more aristocratic and centralizing element which emphasized the need for discipline and federal leadership. And of course its restraining influence, which was an essential part of its work, was often irksome. When the Republicans (who later became the Democrats) gained power, its position was inevitably weakened. There was close voting on the renewal of its charter (65 against to 64 favourable in the House, and 17 to 17 in the Senate), and it lapsed in 1811. There followed immediately a mushroom growth of state banks and of their circulation; this was partly to fill the gap, but went much beyond what was needed, and by 1814 all banks outside New England had suspended payment on their notes.[1] Chaotic conditions quickly supervened, the notes of the various states, and indeed of various towns, standing at different discounts against silver. In fact, the dollar was fast travelling the way of the old shillings, whose differences from one another from colony to colony we have already noted. It is true that those who thought a central bank unnecessary could argue that inflation was excusable and inevitable since war had been declared on England in 1812. But when the war was over, there were no immediate signs of a return to convertibility and the opinion became general that a central bank was needed after all. The second Bank of the United States began operations in 1817 and convertibility was quickly restored. But the old prejudices remained.

It must be taken for granted that President Andrew Jackson had eminent virtues; their sphere of application lies outside my special field of study. From the currency point of view, he may be described simply as a bull in a china shop. In 1832 he vetoed the bill that had been duly passed by Congress for considering the renewal of

[1] The state banks referred to here and subsequently were banks operating under the various laws of their several states, but not in any sense state-owned or state-controlled institutions.

the Bank's charter, which was due to expire in 1836, and shortly afterwards he roughly and rudely withdrew public deposits from the Bank, thus prematurely bringing its operations to a virtual end.

Memory of the two Hamilton banks — the second may be ascribed to him, since it was largely a replica of the first — tends to fade and they seldom receive honourable mention. It is therefore worth noticing that their combined period of operation was as long as the period for which the Federal Reserve System has been in existence to date (1953).

They seem to have done their jobs reasonably well. There were numerous complaints, both that they had overexpanded and that they had shown undue severity. But good heavens! The Bank of England has made mistakes enough in its long history, but we could not have got on without it. Andrew Jackson's veto occurred in the very period in which the Bank of England was subject to the strongest criticism in England, and the great controversy was raging which led eventually to the passage of Peel's Bank Act (1844). These two successive Banks of the United States looked after the public accounts and issued notes, the convertibility of which was successfully sustained. The state banks also issued notes. These were accepted in payment by the Bank of the United States. Its mode of enforcing discipline was from time to time to send round bundles of state bank notes to the state banks for them to convert. Having regard to the fact that at that time notes played the part in the circulation subsequently played by cheques drawn on deposits, this method may be deemed to correspond precisely, although being a little more arbitrary, to the action of the Federal Reserve Banks in requesting member banks to reduce their indebtedness.

All sorts of miscellaneous accusations were levelled against the Bank of the United States, often quite fatuous. The charge that was most frequently made at a high level was that it altogether failed to provide the country with a decent currency. In so far as this refers to the coinage, which was indeed deplorable, it may be said that this was quite outside the power and province of a central bank. The causes of the disorders in the coinage have already been discussed. It was also complained that notes and drafts were only accepted at a discount if presented in a distant part of the country. The Bank had failed to establish what in the language of a later time was known as par clearance. This is hardly surprising, when we consider what a heavy and difficult task the Federal Reserve System found it to establish par clearance in an age when transport and communications had so greatly improved. Indeed, par clearance was not achieved without much highly unpopular pressure and litigation.

The suspension of the second Bank was in its turn quickly followed by another mushroom growth of state banks and by a general suspension of the convertibility of notes (1837). This time there was no foreign war to provide an excuse for the disorders. Gallatin, writing in 1841,[1] ascribes them to the suspension of the central bank, and we may suppose that his diagnosis was correct. The period of inconvertibility lasted fairly continuously for five years. Thereafter the Californian gold output came along to make it easier for the convertibility of a rapidly expanding note issue to be maintained. But local patches of inconvertibility occurred from time to time.

When the Civil War broke out, the Federal authorities, despite some doubt on the constitutional question, issued notes, the famous 'greenbacks'. This time the exigencies did provide an ample and genuine excuse for inflation. The United States had an inconvertible paper currency from 1862 to 1879. When the war was over

[1] *Suggestions on the Banks and Currency*, 1841.

there were hopes of an early return to specie payments, a moderate deflation was undertaken and the issue of greenbacks was reduced from 431 to 356 million. The deflation naturally gave rise to discontent, and after 1868 there was no further reduction, and indeed before 1879 there was a slight increase. The total amount of paper in circulation decreased till 1867, but thereafter increased fairly continuously. The expansionist tendencies overmastered the desire of the authorities to return to a specie standard; the authorities may have been wise in not pressing the question too hard. George S. Bootwell became Secretary of the Treasury under Grant in 1869, and is quoted by Hepburn [1] as holding that 'as Congress and the country were opposed to contraction, the only alternative to bring about resumption was to await the increased need for circulation by the natural growth of population and business'. This may have been a sensible view. Dare we take it as a precedent for Britain to-day? Her struggle against Hitler may perhaps be compared in intensity with the American Civil War, the strain and burdens of which must not be underrated. By this analogy, Britain should be expected to restore sterling convertibility in 1959. If we may press the analogy even further, Congress finally enacted the restoration of convertibility in 1875, naming 1879 as the date for its coming into operation. This would give Britain until 1955 to make its final decision, with a further four years' grace thereafter to bring the thing into effect.

The Civil War was the occasion for a revision of the banking system in the United States. 'National' banks were instituted, to operate under federal law, as distinct from the state banks which operated under the varied state laws. The national banks were authorized to issue notes based on specified classes of government bonds, while the state banks' issues were eliminated by the

[1] A. B. Hepburn, *History of Coinage and Currency in the United States*, p. 218.

imposition of penal taxation. Uniform reserve requirements were imposed upon the national banks.

Branch banking continued to be prohibited. Banks
in outlying parts or smaller towns held reserves in banks
in the larger towns and these in turn held reserves in
still more central cities, notably New York. The special
responsibility of the large banks was recognized by the
designation of certain cities as 'reserve' cities and others
as 'central reserve' cities and the requirement of higher
reserve ratios in these cities. It was thought that in this
way the large banks would between them fulfil the
function of holding central reserves, which was fulfilled
by the central banks of other countries. It was thus
believed by many that there would never be any need
for an obnoxious central bank. But the great banks did
not really play their essential part. Required reserves
were calculated on a percentage system; the central
reserve city banks, being required by law to hold larger
reserves, did so; but on a percentage system required
reserves are not available for use; being required by
law to hold more than others, these banks did not feel
it incumbent upon themselves to hold more still, and
hence, in a crisis, no spare gold was available to meet
drains from up-country.

The consequence was that there were too many
crises. England had her last really serious crisis in 1866
— an event not altogether unconnected with the end of
the Civil War; further crises were prevented by the
smooth working of the Bank of England under Bagehot's
precepts. But the United States continued to be racked
by violent crises, that of 1893 being of exceptional severity
— hence Bryan's large number of votes in 1896 — and
that of 1907 hardly less so. Distress and needless
suffering occurred on these occasions. To prevent an
absolute and universal standstill, the large banks joined
together to issue what were known as Clearing House
Loan Certificates. Although not strictly notes, they

served the purpose of notes, and were therefore in effect emergency issues outside the legal provision. Thus the issue of these Loan Certificates may be regarded as the precise equivalent of the issue of the notes in Britain after the suspension of Peel's Bank Act. But whereas Peel's Bank Act only had to be suspended three times, the last in 1866, Clearing House Loan Certificates had to be issued on ten occasions prior to the foundation of the Federal Reserve System.

The national bank-note issue was somewhat inelastic, being based on low interest U.S. bonds rather than bills of trade, but in the last quarter of the nineteenth century the expansionists concentrated their energies upon the silver question.

Throughout the nineteenth century U.S. currency had its double aspect. On the whole, the system did provide the base of a vast industrial and agricultural expansion. In the earlier period, the notes were provided by state banks; the coinage remained disorderly and much inconvertibility of notes was tolerated. Later the national banks replaced the state banks in the note-issuing capacity, and in that were more conservative. The state banks continued their other banking business. As in the period following Peel's Bank Act in England, the growing use of cheques circumvented the limitations which would otherwise have been due to restrictive currency regulations. But while expansion went forward, the United States was plagued with severe crises, and it can hardly be doubted that this was due to the absence of a central bank, which can on the one hand exert a moderating influence on expansion, and on the other bring quick and healing relief when a crisis comes. In the United States there was no method of organizing a restraining influence, and, for the reasons stated above, there was no central reserve.

It is to be emphasized that despite the gold crucifixion and despite the somewhat restricted currency, the expansion in the last quarter of the century was vast, and it was in this period that the United States established her industrial leadership. At the same time, her foreign trade rapidly expanded. Before the mid-seventies she had had a passive balance on her external current account, attracting foreign capital to fill the gap. From that time onwards she has sustained a considerable excess of exports over imports. In view of our current problems, it might be interesting for me to close this lecture by giving figures for her visible balance of trade.

EXCESS OF EXPORTS FROM U.S. OVER IMPORTS INTO U.S.

	(i) $ Million	(ii) As per cent. of Exports
1880	158	15
1885	149	20·5
1890	56	6·6
1895	62	7·8
1900	52·2	38·1
1905	374	25·1
1910	154	9
1920–24 (av.)	1305	27·7
1924–9 (av.)	819	16·2
1933–8 (av.)	338	13
1946–8 (av.)	6279	45·5
1950–52 (av.)	1915*	15·5

* Including exports financed by aid except military end-items.

In the early part of this period, the excess of exports was offset partly by invisible payments on current account and partly by the redemption of investments previously made in the United States by foreigners. The only period in which she undertook large foreign investments of her own was in the decade after the First World War. From the 1890s until the Second World War gold, newly mined in South Africa, played an important part in closing the gap.

This gap exercises us very much to-day. It is often supposed that it is a new phenomenon due to developments since the Second World War. While there have recently been various factors tending to increase the excess of exports by the United States, it is to be noted that the big change occurred three-quarters of a century ago, and that ever since the United States has had a substantial surplus on visible trade account. What is new in the present situation is not this surplus, but the disappearance of the ways in which it has heretofore been met. Recognition of this should affect our thinking about the current dollar problem. If the trading deficit of the rest of the world with the United States was mainly due to overspending on post-war reconstruction, or to undisciplined inflations, the correctives required would be fairly clearly marked out for us. To alter a pattern that has existed for three-quarters of a century is not so easy.

II

THE FEDERAL RESERVE SYSTEM

In retrospect, it seems clear enough that the United States was in sore need of some kind of central banking organization. Other mature countries had developed one; the proper functions of such an organization were well defined; its value was urged by theoretical and practical experts on the subject; the adverse experience of the United States in successive financial crashes confirmed the need. It might have been thought that the severe troubles of 1893 would have sufficed to stimulate action. But we have seen that the discontents engendered by that crisis found vent in Bryan's great silver campaign. The Spanish War came to distract attention. The Republicans, having defeated Bryan by a narrow margin in 1896 on a 'sound money' plan, deferred action until the eleventh hour (1900), and then merely produced a measure which on the one hand reaffirmed the gold standard and on the other liberalized the conditions for the formation of national banks. This contributed nothing to the main problem and might indeed be deemed to have increased the dangers of unhealthy boom.

By the turn of the century the 1893 crisis seems to have spent its force as a stimulant to action. Mention must, however, be made of continuing work by Charles Fowler, as Chairman of the House Committee on Banking and Currency, which resulted in a contribution to the stock of ideas that could be drawn upon when the reform eventually came.

Measures of monetary reconstruction seem particularly hard to achieve; in most cases complex monetary systems and institutions have evolved by gradual stages from simple origins, adaptation following adaptation to meet the practical needs of the moment. Public opinion, whether popular or informed, appears to be somewhat allergic to monetary reform. It is, after all, a difficult subject, and dry as dust. The ordinary man feels an inferiority complex in the face of these problems, and therefore tends to be repelled by them and to dismiss them from his mind. One might expect, therefore, that it would be difficult to create a central banking system *ab ovo* in a highly complex economy, such as the United States had long since become. Special characteristics of Americans added to the difficulties, their intense individualism, their resistance to centralizing tendencies and their suspicion of bankers and high finance, which smelt too much for their liking of the bad old world. From the point of view of politicians having an eye to popularity, this central banking question was clearly one to be taken up only under extreme necessity. And so the new century saw a period of further drift.

But then came the crash of 1907. Once again an impetus was given, and this time it proved sufficient.

The history of the origins of the Federal Reserve System, which officially came into being in 1914, is somewhat tangled. There were strong political cross-currents. Distinguished men who took part in those events and afterwards wrote about them have not steered altogether clear of partisanship. In practical, as in scientific, matters questions of priority often involve fine nuances. On the road between a mere crude suggestion and a fully-fledged scheme, it is not always easy to say who infused the original thought. I would not presume from a distance to make the delicate judgements required for the full story, and will confine myself to two or three facts which stand out clearly.

Mention must first be made of the crucial work of Nelson W. Aldrich. At this time he had acquired a dominant, and indeed supreme, position in the Senate as an authority on monetary questions. This was based on his integrity and eminence of character, his grasp of principle, and his meticulous attention to practical detail. Soon after the crisis of 1907, he produced a bill providing for the issue of emergency notes on critical occasions. A bill of similar character had been put forward in the House by E. B. Vreeland, and, after the usual conference, the Aldrich-Vreeland Act emerged. The Act also contained a provision of much greater importance, namely, for the setting up of a National Monetary Commission, to consist of members of the Senate and the House. Of this Commission, Aldrich became chairman. It laboured over a number of years, producing much information which was embodied in thirty-five volumes. Reformers could not at first pin high hopes to its work, since Aldrich had always expressed firm opposition to the idea of a central bank.

At an early stage in its labours (1908), the Commission visited Europe to enquire into central banking practice on the spot. Nelson Aldrich's quality of practical good sense manifested itself. He was impressed by the obvious value of these European institutions and their smoothly working relations with the great commercial banks. Paul Warburg vividly describes his first meeting with Aldrich after his return:

'Mr. Warburg,' he said quietly, 'I like your ideas. I have only one fault to find with them.'

This intimation that the Senator had been won over to the central reserve doctrine came like a thunderbolt from a clear sky; but I asked, with as great composure as I could command, what that fault was.

He answered, 'You are too timid about it.'

This was an even more intense surprise to me than his first statement, and I replied that, so far, it had appeared to me that I was almost the only person in the banking reform movement who had shown any courage about it.

He said, 'Yes, but you say we cannot have a central bank, and I say we can.'

It is easy to imagine, but hard to describe, the mixed feelings of joy and bewilderment into which this remark threw me.[1]

The consequence of Aldrich's conversion was that the National Monetary Commission produced a plan for a National Reserve Association, which came very near to being a central bank; this became known as the Aldrich Plan. Furthermore, Aldrich embarked upon a campaign of persuasion and in due course converted many bankers to his point of view. This was a crucial episode in the story. It would in any case be hard enough to get the American public to agree to a brand new centralized banking organization; if the bankers did not want it themselves, that would clearly increase the difficulty. Aldrich, owing to his position of unique authority, was able to do more than any other could have done in causing a change of view in those quarters, and he must thus be credited with having made an essential contribution to the good cause.

Here in England we derive comfort at this time from having among us Mr. Winthrop Aldrich, distinguished son of a distinguished father. He is here on a mission too, albeit of a somewhat different kind. Is it possible that he too will gain a closer knowledge of certain facts that can lead to a change of mind, and that he will be able to go home, like his father before him, bearer of a fruitful idea that could be of benefit both to his country and to the world? Far be it from me to specify precisely the topic or issue in regard to which such a 'conversion' might be helpful! I merely throw it out as a challenge to this generation. Have we something to contribute, as did our fathers forty-five years ago, that might be of value to the economies on both sides of the Atlantic? Or are we in this generation

[1] P. Warburg, *The Federal Reserve System*, vol. i, p. 56.

bankrupt of ideas? That is for Mr. Winthrop Aldrich to ascertain.

But Nelson Aldrich was not destined to bring his own particular plan to fruition. In consequence of the elections of 1910, the Democrats obtained control of the House and thereby of the House Banking and Currency Committee. Nelson Aldrich might labour in the good cause among bankers and men of business, but the Democrats were likely to have different ideas. Who knew what would happen in the Presidential Election of 1912? The first idea of the Democrats in the House was to have an all-out onslaught on the 'Money Trust'. Into the nature of that sinister monster we need not enquire. Such a 'muckraking' excursion is congenial to certain elements in the American character. I often remember finding myself in one glorious spring many years later the neighbour in Alassio of an American of venerable mien. He was living in an Italian villa with a beautiful garden amid mountains clad in olive trees and looking out upon the blue waters of the Mediterranean. One day he handed me a tastefully printed card, which was a notice, or one might say a blurb, of a book he had recently written, under the title *Moses in Red*. On the card was inscribed his own name, Mr. Lincoln Steffens, and under it the words 'the world's greatest muckrake'. When I had overcome my initial surprise that such a venerable figure should so describe himself, I reflected that this was after all a highly honourable and most beneficial profession. While not disputing Mr. Steffens's claim to the world title, I may remind you that we English have had a strong candidate for it in the person of Henry Labouchère, a man highly regarded in Victorian England.

Clearly this offensive against the Money Trust was an exciting matter, and Mr. Pujo, chairman by seniority of the House Committee, was anxious to get on with the job that was much more interesting than the dry-as-dust questions that were being concurrently pondered by the National Monetary Commission. It was decided to let the House Committee be divided into two sub-committees; naturally the Money Trust would have to be handled by the senior sub-committee. And so by this accident it happened that Mr. Carter Glass became chairman of the enquiry into the central banking question. Here, amid the hurly-burly of the Democratic party fresh to power, which had its wild and irresponsible elements, was a man especially fitted to educate the party on the more austere aspects of this subject. His careful study, hard work, dogged pertinacity and skill in complicated negotiations have been highly praised by his contemporaries. He enlisted the services of H. Parker Willis as expert assistant; [1] Glass attributes to Willis the initiative in proposing at a late stage the all-important section on open-market operations.[2] Glass approached the problem by working out a scheme for a chain of regional banks which should perform central banking functions, each in its own region.[3]

The Presidential campaign of 1912 was not encouraging for monetary reformers. The reference by the Taft Republicans was very anaemic; the Roosevelt Republicans actually declared their opposition to the Aldrich plan; the Democrats declared opposition to 'the Aldrich plan or a central bank'.[4]

But now a new figure appeared on the scene. There are no doubt disadvantages in having a don in a position of supreme power; another don, the late Lord Keynes, has argued that Woodrow Wilson was inadequately equipped to handle those seasoned political veterans,

[1] Parker Willis's massive treatise entitled *The Federal Reserve System* is injured by needless partisanship.

[2] C. Glass, *Adventure in Constructive Finance*, p. 93.

[3] V. Morawetz had earlier produced proposals on regional lines.

[4] It has beer suggested, with what plausibility I know not, that a malign type-setter dropped an 'f' from the fourth word in the expression quoted.

Clemenceau and Lloyd George. But in the sphere of banking reform, a don was just what was wanted. A professor is not repelled, but attracted, by the dry-as-dust character of a subject. Wilson had the mental grasp to understand that this banking question, albeit abstract and recondite, was fundamental, and that if he could achieve a good measure, he would be doing something really constructive, which would be of lasting credit to his administration. And so in the event it has proved.

Glass, who had been continuing in his labours, was anxious to know how the President-elect would view them, and secured an interview as early as December 26, 1913, at Princeton. Woodrow Wilson proved to be not only sound, but keen, on this question. Till that interview, no one among the many who had been doing hard work in research or propaganda was quite sure that anything would result, that he was not battling with complete unrealities. The campaign of 1912 had very much suggested that. The great mass of public opinion remained hostile, or at best, apathetic. When the attitude of the new President was ascertained, the whole scene was transformed. The reformers took courage. Glass records that Wilson was interested to know what the centralizing force would be to give coherence to the regional banks. In the Glass plan the Comptroller of the Currency had this rôle. Wilson suggested a 'Board'.[1] Thus he may be deemed to be the originator of the Federal Reserve Board (since vexatiously renamed Board of Governors of the Federal Reserve System). But that was not his only contribution. Throughout the stormy passage that followed, the President's firm support was indispensable, and to him must be accorded a large part of the credit for the existence of the Federal Reserve System.

Among his supporters, and in his Cabinet as Secretary of State, was that famous figure W. J. Bryan,

[1] Glass, *Adventure in Constructive Finance*, p. 82.

seasoned and mellowed no doubt by now, but still a forceful radical. He was likely to have great influence with those Democrats who would be most hostile to bankers and centralization. He gained from the President two concessions that he deemed to be of primary importance, in return for which he gave his loyal support to the measure thereafter. Of these, one was that the Federal Reserve notes were to be obligations of the United States. Much was made of this concession, which was deemed to be of profound significance, not only by Bryan and his followers, but also by the conservatives, who repeatedly cited it as a reason for opposing the whole measure. In the history of the Federal Reserve System to date, I am not aware that the fact of these notes being legally United States obligations has made the smallest difference in any practical problem that has arisen. In fact this concession was one of null content. The President showed his cunning here. If he had not that quality in sufficient measure to defeat the wiles of Lloyd George, it was, at least, sufficient for this occasion. Glass quotes him as follows : 'If we can hold to the substance of the thing and give the other fellow the shadow, why not do it, if thereby we may save the bill ?' [1]

The other concession was of much greater importance. The Board, instead of being appointed by the community of bankers and consisting mainly of bankers, was to be appointed by the President. It was greatly feared that this would make the Federal Reserve System a mere tool in the hands of successive politicians. This, too, was made a prime reason for opposition by the conservatives. Of course, all depended on the President's choice and the precedent established by the early nominations. The concession may have been a wise one, since it gained the support not only of Bryan, but also of a far wider range of public opinion which might

[1] Glass, *op. cit.* p. 125.

otherwise have feared that the community was being sold out to the bankers. Wilson no doubt had it in mind that he would appoint some bankers to the Board, as he did; I am not fully competent to judge on this matter, but I understand that on the whole his appointments were of a character to set a good precedent, and that he might feel that this concession to 'radicalism' also could be purged of ill-effects.

And so the measure went forward. It was in the nick of time. The National Banking System had had to be created in the midst of the Civil War. The more majestic edifice of the Federal Reserve System was already in being in time to cope with the mighty problems created by the First World War.

The Federal Reserve did not prevent a strong inflation developing during the First World War; but neither did the Bank of England. By too strong a deflationary policy, it may have intensified the post-war depression; the Bank of England acted similarly. We cannot doubt that the troubles would have been far more severe if the United States had had to face the vast strains of war without a central banking organization.

Amid the varied problems and interesting developments of the System, I can only select one or two points for mention.

Of the arguments in favour of a central banking system, the strongest was the need for a central reserve. This was generally recognized. Of equal weight in the minds of the planners was the need to have an 'elastic' currency based on commercial paper. Of the validity of this we may be more doubtful. While there was naturally great stress on the need to mitigate the evils of crisis, surprisingly little was said during the preliminary discussions of the duty of a central bank to curb expansion during the preceding boom. There is an intriguing parallel with the discussions prior to Bretton Woods, where thought was concentrated on how an international institution might aid in mitigating a slump such as that of 1929–33, and little was heard of its proper functions in a period of world-wide inflation. An 'elastic' currency has its dangers. It may be granted that the prior system by which the backing for national bank-notes was confined to a narrow class of 2 per cent. government bonds worked perversely. One could remedy this either by enlarging the class of securities on which notes could be based, or by introducing commercial bills, and American opinion was divided on this issue, but the latter view gained ascendancy. It was thought that this would enable the note issue to conform itself to the expanding needs of commerce from time to time; yet this may not be altogether sound doctrine. It may be observed that no appreciable part of the Bank of England issue is normally backed by commercial paper, except for critical short periods when 'the market is in the Bank'.

I must be allowed to dwell for a few minutes on these technical matters, since they have far-reaching consequences; they affect the general character of the United States banking system, and thereby of the dollar, and are even relevant to the intractability of the 'dollar gap' at the present time.

Bound up with the question of backing notes by commercial paper was the view, stressed especially by such bankers as Paul Warburg, that a great trading country like the United States ought to have her own independent market for acceptances, and that such a market was needful for the good working of a central banking institution. It was an essential part of the British mechanism. Attempts were accordingly made to develop such a market, and, with this in view, the Federal Reserve System stood ready to purchase any number of acceptances offered to it in the open market; but for this offer to encourage the drawing of acceptances, it was needful for the Federal Reserve Banks to be willing to take up any residue of acceptances at the market rate of interest, which might be expected to be, and normally was, below the official rediscount rates of the Federal Reserve Banks. But this very concession, which could hardly be avoided until there was an independent acceptance market standing on its own legs, made the mode of operation of the System entirely different from that of the Bank of England, and reduced its power of control. In the classic period of the 'twenties, the market for acceptances never became fully independent, and the system of the double rate had to be maintained.

It sometimes used to be said in treatises, that whereas the Bank of England rate was normally above the market rate and thereby a penalty rate, the Federal Reserve rates for rediscount were below the market. This was not strictly accurate, since the markets in question were for different kinds of paper. It was natural and proper that the Federal Reserve rates for rediscount should be below the market rates on one-name paper (called bills in United States terminology); the mere fact that such paper had passed through a member bank on its way to rediscount raised its status and entitled it to a lower rate. The official Federal Reserve rates for rediscount were *above* the market rates on paper equivalent to British bills of exchange, namely, acceptances. The real difference between the two systems lay not in the different levels of their official rediscount rates compared with market rates on comparable paper — for there was no such difference — but in the existence of that supplementary (lower) rate offered by the Federal Reserve Banks on acceptances. This in turn was not due to misguided policy, but to the necessities of the case; for if the Federal Reserve System had not maintained these differential rates, there was a full probability that the acceptance market, which it was trying to create, would wither away again. The London discount market has become inured through the course of generations to discounting at very low rates; it was not easy to persuade Americans, who had become habituated to getting a better return on loose money, that the return on acceptances was adequate.

Tied up with this problem was the use of member banks' call money for loans to stock-market brokers. It was well known that British call money went to discount houses, which used it for discounting acceptances, and that this application of liquid funds provided the Bank of England with the leverage by which it controlled money market rates. When it sold securities in the open market and squeezed its 'member' banks,[1] they called in call money and compelled the discount market to borrow from the Bank of England at a penalty rate. Some hoped that in the United States member bank call money might gradually be diverted to the acceptance market, but this hope was not realized. Paradoxically the requirement for daily settlement in the American stock markets, which was intended to prevent speculation, actually encouraged it. Fortnightly settlement gave British speculators some scope, but in the United States, where this was lacking, the habit of getting brokers to put up part of the money had become firmly established, and consequently the demand by the brokers for call money from the banks was firm and continuous. Some thought that the Federal Reserve should seek to change this system, but nothing was done for the time being, and a different solution was found in the 'thirties.

When the Bank of England imposes an open market squeeze, the impact is upon that section of the total money market which normally lends money at a rate below Bank Rate, and for which therefore the Bank Rate is a penalty rate. Since this market has to get out

[1] I adopt Keynes' proposal in so describing our British banks. 'The typical modern Banking System consists of a Sun, namely the Central Bank, and Planets, which, following American usage, it is convenient to call the Member Banks' (*Treatise on Money*, vol. i, p. 9).

of debt with the Bank of England as quickly as possible, the effect of the squeeze is to cause a net reduction in the cash basis of the monetary system by the full amount of the open market sales, and, if the sales are sufficiently substantial, an increase in the money market rates of discount. All this happens within a matter of days. In the case of the Federal Reserve System, member banks restore their position in the first instance, not by calling in call money, but by increasing their rediscounts with their Federal Reserve Banks — always supposing that their reserves initially are not in excess. The Federal Reserve Bank rates are not, for the reasons already stated, above the average rates earned by the member banks on their earning assets, and may not be above the rate earned by any part of those assets. Consequently, there is no urgent need for them to get out of debt within a matter of days. It does not follow that the Federal Reserve action is ineffective. Member banks dislike being in debt for long, and, if they show indifference about this, the Federal Reserve Banks can in due course put pressure upon individual members. There will be a tendency over a period of time for the member banks to strive to reduce their indebtedness, and therefore to pursue a tighter lending policy. In the long run, the tight credit policy becomes effective. But the process is much slower than in the British system. One might say that the Federal Reserve control is less sharp.

It does not follow that their system is inferior. Rather we should think of it as adapted to a different situation. For the Bank of England in the period we are discussing the first and foremost consideration was the external balance. The British external payments were somewhat larger in absolute amount, and far larger relatively to national income and to the volume of the internal circulating medium, than the American; and the British system was managed on the basis of an extremely narrow central gold reserve. It was therefore essential that upon the advent of an adverse turn in the external balance, a very quick remedy should be available; this remedy was found in the impact of tighter credit upon short-term capital movements. In the United States not only was the volume of external payments a much smaller item in the national economy, but also from 1921 onwards the central gold reserve was vast in relation to possible discrepancies in the external balance. Indeed at times the gold reserve was so large as to be a cause of embarrassment, as, for example, in 1923. Consequently, the Federal Reserve System was in a position to be relatively indifferent about the state of the external balance. It was free to concentrate its attention upon the effect of its credit policy upon the internal economy.

While this difference raises interesting problems in regard to the internal effects of central banking policy, the external reaction must be noted. The British had the need and means to correct an adverse external development quickly. There was also the other side of the case. A favourable development usually entailed a speedy easing of credit and a strong encouragement to international lending. Britain maintained her policy of a narrow gold reserve, and any tendency to accumulation was quickly countered by a stimulus to foreign borrowing from London. Thus, in the normal course, no 'oppressive' creditor position was maintained for long, and there was no continuing pull upon the liquid resources of other countries. There was no such need and no such consequence in the United States; a net credit position on the over-all external account could continue indefinitely.

We must by no means jump to the conclusion that the U.S. policy was negligent of the good-neighbour principle. If the Federal Reserve authorities regarded it as their duty to give primary attention to maintaining steady credit conditions inside the United States, this was of value to the whole world. It may well have been much more important to the world that steady business conditions should prevail in the United States, than that the United States should have a relatively even balance on external account. If the effect of the American system might be to cause a continuing drain of gold from other countries, this was due, not to a failure of authorities to recognize their true duty, but to the very nature of the case. This case does not call for any reproaches against the United States authorities, but for a deeper study as to how the wise management of the internal credit structure can be combined with avoiding an oppressive continuance of an unduly favourable balance on over-all external account. Before considering this, we must examine the question of internal policy more closely.

The year 1923 was notable in two respects. It saw a turning-point in U.S. monetary policy, and it gave rise to the publication by the Federal Reserve Board of its classic Tenth Annual Report, viz. for 1923, published in 1924. This is one of the most important documents in world monetary history. It has to be admitted that a number of its propositions are open to question, and the Federal Reserve Board would no doubt have wished to rewrite some parts quite differently a few years later. But it contains much that endures, and it presented a new philosophy of central banking management which was destined to be the background, and to supply the implicit pre-conceptions, of all future discussions of policy.

The United States had endured the inflation of war and a severe post-war deflation; and then, in 1922, it appeared to many that a new bout of inflation was under way. It was welcome that industry was recovering from the severe depression of 1920–21; by 1923 employment was reported as being very full. But it was important that recovery should not develop into a renewed inflationary spiral, and this was feared. Between the first quarter of 1922 and the first quarter of 1923, general prices rose 12 per cent.

Between October 1920 and April 1922 rediscounts with the Federal Reserve System fell from $2801 million in October 1920 to $510 million in April 1922.[1] This was partly associated with the fall of prices, and partly caused by the great inflow of gold into the United States in 1921, which provided a cash basis for the member banks alternative to that acquired by rediscounting. While rediscounts fell, 'bills bought in the open market' also fell, from $298 million to $90 million. These bills do not reflect the active open market policy of the System, the transactions in question being on the initiative of the market in accordance with the Federal Reserve offer, given for reasons already stated, to mop up surplus acceptances not absorbed by the market. The Federal Reserve Banks accordingly found themselves somewhat short of earning assets, and it was not unnatural that their holdings of United States securities — this being the item due to Federal Reserve initiative — were increased from $296 million to $587 million. It was recognized to be of some, though not paramount, importance that the Federal Reserve Banks should pay their way. How far was this purchasing policy to be continued? How far was it self-defeating owing to the fact that the more the Federal Reserve Banks purchased through this channel, the more the member banks were inclined to reduce rediscounts? These matters began to be deeply considered in 1922, and in April of that year a committee of officers to execute open market policy was appointed. It is not clear how early opinion, under the leadership of such men as Mr. Miller and Benjamin Strong, began to crystallize. The Open Market Committee, on which the larger Federal Reserve Banks were represented, was given greater responsibility

[1] Ninth Annual Report of the Federal Reserve Board.

in April 1923, and it is to the spring of that year that a definite policy of unloading U.S. securities is usually assigned. A reduction in holdings had already been proceeding from mid-1922, being reduced from $603 million to $436 million at the end of the year, but this reduction may have been but the natural reaction to a corresponding increase in open market acceptances. In 1923 the holding of U.S. securities was further reduced to $98 million by the end of July, despite the fact that open-market acceptances fell slightly. So far as open-market policy was concerned, the first half of 1923 period must be regarded as a period of strong deflation. What is to be noted is that throughout this period the Federal Reserve Banks held more than double the gold that they were required to hold by law, round about 77 per cent. of notes and deposit combined as against the 40 per cent. required to back notes and the 35 per cent. required to back deposit liabilities. At the same time, gold coming into the country was deliberately being kept out of the Federal Reserve System by the Treasury issue of gold certificates. As these could at any time be replaced by Federal Reserve notes, the true gold reserve was considerably above 77 per cent. Thus we have the phenomenon of strong open market deflation at a time when the Federal Reserve System held what was probably a higher ratio of gold than any central bank had ever enjoyed. The deflation was required solely by the internal situation. Thus credit policy had been completely divorced from the external situation. And who shall say that this was wrong? It was not in the interest of the world, any more than that of the United States herself, that a new bout of inflation should develop in the United States. The famous Tenth Report describes this policy diplomatically, but none the less with precision; 'the gradual withdrawal from the open market by the Reserve banks during the first half of 1923 placed upon the member banks the responsibility for validating the continued use of the existing volume of Reserve bank credit'.

The authors of the Tenth Annual Report state fairly and squarely that it is the duty of the Federal Reserve System, in accordance with the terms of the Act which established it, to maintain steady credit conditions in the country. While each Federal Reserve Bank may do what it can by way of qualitative supervision, to ensure that individual member banks do not use credit for speculation or other undesirable purposes, it is recognized that the main weapon of a central banking system for preventing speculative development must be by an over-all policy in regard to the total quantity of central reserve credit vouchsafed to the economy. Those restraints, so markedly absent in the United States in the nineteenth century and so little discussed prior to 1914, were now in effective operation. In 1922–3, the Federal Reserve System applied a brake to the gathering boom, which might otherwise have led to a crisis like those of 1893 and 1907.

The Report discusses what was to be the criterion for the new-found policy. It rejects the notion of a stable general price level on two grounds, namely (1) that it was not practicable for the System to guarantee a stable general price level, and (2) that, if expansive or restrictive action was only taken after prices had begun to move downwards or upwards, it would often be action taken too late. The System should be able to do better than that. Later in the decade there was an agitation for the legal enforcement of a policy of a rigidly stable general price level, and a measure was introduced by James Strong — not to be confused with the great Benjamin — in Congress, and fully discussed in committee; but it was not passed.

The Report offers an alternative criterion for policy, which we need not consider wholly satisfactory. It holds that all is well if consumption is in even balance with production, any tendency towards an accumulation of inventories being a symptom of undue expansion. But it is clear from the general tenor of the Report that all possible indices of over-expansion or depression will be carefully watched, and that it is to be the object of credit policy to secure a steady advance of the economy. For this purpose, the fact that open market operations have slower working effects than in England was no great handicap, or even conceivably an advantage.

The Report does not pass over without comment the point that the external balance, involving an inflow or outflow of gold, might have been expected to afford the normal criterion for credit policy; its authors show awareness that their proposals for divorcing credit policy from this criterion are in effect revolutionary. An apology is made for this departure from the older doctrine. The excuse given is that the international gold standard was not in operation at this time, owing to the fact that most countries were still off the gold standard; consequently a gold inflow could no longer be accepted as a meaningful criterion for credit policy by the sole important gold standard country. There may have been some truth in this, although the argument is not wholly satisfying. There does seem to be an implication in the Report that if and when most other countries returned to the gold standard, there would be a reversion to the more orthodox criterion. But although there is this implication in the strict logic of the wording of certain paragraphs, no one can read this Report as a whole without the conviction that its authors regard any such reversion as merely a remote hypothesis, and are firmly determined to carry into practice the new ideas over a considerable period. And so it happened. I do not think that since 1923 Federal Reserve credit policy has ever been governed by the international gold standard criterion, except for a sidelong glance in 1927, and even then the policy in question could be justified on internal grounds alone. It may be said on the other side that even after most other countries had returned to the gold standard, they did not observe over-nicely the rules of the international gold standard game; this fact might be deemed to exempt the Federal Reserve System from the duty to change its ways.

It must be repeated, and with emphasis, that the Federal Reserve is not to be criticized for its new departure. And by this I do not merely mean that it was entitled to give priority to the needs of the American economy as against international equilibrium. It is by no means clear that its new-found policy was detrimental to the international equilibrium. A great economy, such as the United States, may affect economies abroad in three principal ways. (1) If it is out of balance on current and capital accounts, its attraction of gold may create embarrassment elsewhere. Much stress has been laid on this, and it has its importance. (2) Changes in the volume and value of its imports may have more important external effects than changes in its balance. A great shrinkage in the orders that it places abroad may have a depressing effect with cumulative repercussions on the economies of other countries, even although its balance of payments remains even and it is not attracting gold. (3) The shrinkage of activity in such an economy may do harm, not merely by the reduction in the orders that it places abroad, but by causing a world-wide fall in the price level of international commodities and a shrinkage of the incomes of their producers, which may be far greater than the loss of income due to the loss of orders, and have more devastating effects. By trying to maintain steadiness in the American economy, the Federal Reserve System was *eo ipso* trying to save the world from adverse repercussions under the second and third heads, and, since such adverse repercussions could do much more harm than the imbalance referred to under the first head, it may be concluded that this pioneering attempt by the Federal Reserve System was not inimical to world interests. The trouble was that in due course the attempt proved unsuccessful.

But that is not quite all that there is to be said. However much we may praise the Federal Reserve for its bold new policy, the fact remains that it did imply a break with the old gold standard system. This was not necessarily to be deplored. At that very time Keynes was inveighing against the gold standard for those very consequences from which the Federal Reserve was, for different causes and reasons, successfully exempting the United States. Keynes was fully alive to the virtues of the delicate mechanism managed by the Bank of England, by which an imbalance of external payments, whether favourable or unfavourable, was speedily corrected. But he argued that the essential working of that mechanism may have had detrimental internal effects from time to time, for example by creating massive unemployment. While there has been sharp criticism, not least in America, of the British subscription to a policy of full employment since the Second World War regardless of whether this involves a risk of having to take measures not fully in accord with the gold standard game, it must be observed that the United States put into operation to the best of her ability a full employment policy in 1923 regardless of its effects upon the international equilibrium. What remains to be said is not that this was wrong, but that the implications for the international equilibrium have not been fully explored to the present day. Fundamental thinking remains to be done; Keynes himself never really tackled this problem.

The policy was executed with seeming success for a period of some six years. Industry and trade grew and prospered in the United States; it seemed that the economy was being kept on an even keel. Only in 1928 did certain unhealthy symptoms appear. The active initiatives of the System are reflected in the variations in its open market holdings of U.S. securities. From a low of $90 million in August 1923 they rose to $588 million in November 1924, fell to $328 million in October 1925, rose to $408 million in June 1926, fell to $291 million in May 1927, rose to $606 million in December 1927, and had been reduced to $153 million by May 1929. These changes were made in response to moderate tendencies to recession or undue expansion, which were carefully watched by the authorities.

An observation must be made about the substantial increase in the second half of 1927. This was accompanied by a general reduction of rediscount rates from 4 to 3½ per cent. and the classic dispute between the Board and the Reserve Bank of Chicago, when the Board had to exert its authority in bringing Chicago into line with the general policy of the System. It was stated that the easement in this period was designed partly to help the countries of Europe which were struggling with the problems of their restored gold standards. The System had already shown its far-sighted statesmanship by giving generous lines of credit where needed to assist the countries restoring the gold standard. Its action in the second half of 1927 was severely criticized afterwards; there were those who said that this unnecessary regard for the difficulties of foreign countries had upset the apple-cart and was responsible for the disasters of 1929. As against this, it must be stated that the policy of easement was also justified by internal conditions. The index of production and the level of prices both fell in 1927, and there was a marked slackness. The internal situation bore some resemblance to that in 1924, when even bolder expansionary measures were deemed justified. Experts at home and abroad continued to think that the Federal Reserve System was executing its new-found policy with marked efficiency and success. But in 1929 all was changed.

Did the System make some error? Having regard to the evidence at its disposal, it is difficult to bring an indictment. But we may ask a more far-reaching question. Now that we have more evidence and can view the events in perspective can we say that, if it had acted differently, the calamities following 1929 could have been avoided? This question cannot be answered for the simple reason that we still do not know what were the basic causes of the world-wide slump of 1929–33.

First we have to decide whether the most important causes lay within the economy of the United States. It can be argued that the United States was merely the victim of forces originating elsewhere. There were certain signs of recession outside the United States before October 1929. Britain had a minor slump in 1928, from which, however, she recovered. There were hesitations in other countries also, and France had a severe crisis in 1927. From early in 1927 there had been a downward trend in the world level of general prices, but it must be added that this was a gentle trend and may well be judged not to have exceeded the rate justified by normal technical progress. Stocks of certain commodities, notably wheat, were increasing, but this trend was not universal or such as to occasion much alarm.

We must by no means be dogmatic on this subject. Too many people talk about American slumps as if it were perfectly clear why they happened and why they must continue to happen. Nothing in regard to the slump beginning in 1929 is perfectly clear. Yet if one looks at all the figures available, and until some new thought or theory is brought to bear upon the subject, it is straining after paradox to affirm that the slump came to the United States from outside and did not originate there. Such an outside influence would manifest itself above all in a decline in the value of U.S. exports, but there was no such decline until after the stock market broke. I think that we must abide in a provisional conclusion that this particular world slump was one which emanated from the United States.

And what caused it there? That certainly no one knows, and in the absence of knowledge of its causes, it is impossible to make a valid criticism of Federal Reserve policy. In my own thoughts about this matter in subsequent years, I was much influenced by Keynes and have ascribed it to what has since been christened the stagnation hypothesis. I remain provisionally of that opinion. This hypothesis has been much criticized in recent years; it has been contended that current events serve to disprove it. I suggest, on the contrary, that it is premature to revise any judgement that the facts might have suggested before 1939 until we have experienced a post-war period free of demands arising from post-war backlogs and from rearmament. I set out my views upon how the stagnation theory applied in the years 1927–9 in a clear, although much over-simplified, form in a volume entitled *The Trade Cycle* (1936).[1] Briefly my explanation was as follows. The stagnation theory postulates that in a mature economy, such as the United States, investment tends to fall short of the values realized by what people would be disposed to save when reasonably fully and profitably employed. This tendency would normally have begun to manifest itself about 1927, that is, after sufficient time had elapsed for meeting post-war backlogs and after the boom associated with the great expansion of automobiles had spent its force. This means that the amount of value saved would not be taken up by industry and that a depression would set in according to the normal Keynesian analysis. Meanwhile there was proceeding an upward adjustment of stock-market values which, to the extent that it went forward in 1927, was a justified and overdue write-up. As the upward movement got further under way, there

[1] Pp. 209-13.

was an increasing tendency for many citizens to enlarge their consumption in response to capital gains accruing from stock-market speculation on margins, which many treated as a supplementary income. Thus to the normal income of a fully employed economy was added a supplementary income coming in from the stock market. So-called income was thus inflated and spending increased at a rate that justified a somewhat abnormally high level of capital expenditure by industry. These two classes of abnormal expenditure, the overspending by the consumers and the capital expenditure required to meet the excess consumer demand, combined to keep the economy fully employed in the 1927–9 period. But as the stock-market boom proceeded and prices were written up to a level that was only justified by the expectation of still further increases, a position was developed which could not be sustained; for clearly the increases could not go on for ever. Once the general level of stock-market values ceased to increase at the 1927–9 rate, as some time it must, this source of supplementary income would be cut off, consumer expenditure would accordingly be reduced somewhat and therewith the need for the existing rate of industrial capital expansion. In fine, the stock-market boom was a mechanism, albeit a mechanism that could not remain in being, for allowing both consumption and capital expenditure to proceed at a rate that exceeded the normal spending propensities and capital requirements of the economy; the stock-market boom kept the operation of the Keynesian tendency in suspense. This was my method of applying Keynesian theory to the events of 1927–9, and I confess that I have not seen any rational explanation of those events that satisfies me so well.

Whatever explanation one might supply, it was clear that once prices in the stock market reached an untenable level there was bound to be trouble. Expert forecasters continued to minimize the scale of readjustment that would be needed, and to pin hopes on the powers of the Federal Reserve, by making credit very easy, to tide the economy over its troubles when the readjustment came. It is evident, however, that the Federal Reserve System was faced by a grave dilemma. Apart from what was happening in Wall Street, its criteria did not suggest that strong measures of deflation were needed. Commodity prices were not rising nor backlogs accumulating in industry. Unemployment was rather unsatisfactorily high. Within the broad field of industry and commerce there just were not any symptoms of inflation. Nor was the rate of expansion abnormally great. It is wrong to think of the period of the late 'twenties as one of a feverish expansion of the American economy. The rate of expansion was easily surpassed not merely in the abnormal conditions of the Second World War, but also in the post-war period. In the six years from 1923 to 1929, the index of industrial production rose by 18 per cent.[1] In the six years from 1946 to 1952 it rose by 29 per cent.[2] Was the Federal Reserve System to apply a very strong deflationary force to industry and trade with a view to curbing the Wall Street boom? This seemed hardly justified by its own terms of reference, which were to keep industry and trade moving forward steadily. Was it to allow the Wall Street boom to proceed unchecked, knowing that this was bound to bring serious trouble in the end? There seems to be no rational answer to this conundrum.

Of course the Federal Reserve could have broken the Wall Street boom six months or a year earlier, if it had been really minded to do so. Had it done so, the adjustment of values required would have been smaller. Would recovery then have been easier? That depends on our basic analysis of the situation. If we accept the stagnation thesis outlined above, it does

[1] Seventeenth Annual Report of the Federal Reserve Board, p. 215.
[2] Economic Report of the President, January 1953.

not appear that recovery would have been much easier.

It was widely held in the System that something should be done, and in due course a discord developed between the views of the all-important Federal Reserve Bank at New York and the Board at Washington. The former pressed early in 1929 for a further rise in rediscount rates, which then stood at 5 per cent. It argued that this was the only way of curbing Wall Street speculation. The Board hoped to get results by the method of moral suasion, that is, by constantly urging member banks not to allow funds to be used for speculation. The New York Bank pointed out that it is impossible to determine the end use of funds borrowed; all customers might be borrowing for ostensibly trade purposes and yet the money might get round to the stock market; the only effective check was to make the cost of borrowing really high. The discord is typical of the divergence between a business point of view and a civil service point of view. The Board at Washington was much concerned about the unpopularity of a tight credit policy, which would necessarily hit industry and trade, and would be bad for the public relations of the Federal Reserve System. The Bank at New York wanted to get down to the brass tacks of the situation and belittled the efficacy of moral suasion. Each took a typical view. In retrospect we can hardly doubt that New York was correct. But the Washington view prevailed until August, when the New York rate was raised to 6 per cent. This was belated.

According to the interpretation set forth above, and indeed according to most interpretations, the reason why trouble was due to follow a bursting of the Wall Street bubble was that the *demand* for goods both on consumer and capital accounts was bound to be much reduced. There was also another point of view, which held that trouble was likely to come from the alleged fact that the stock market was absorbing ever more of the available credit, and that industry would eventually have to face a crisis due to credit shortage. Those who held this opinion were inclined to stress the sectional approach to the problem, namely to seek a remedy, not so much by restricting the global quantity of credit made available by the System, as by closing up the channels by which such credit as there was flowed into stock-market speculation. It may have been indeed impossible, as New York argued that it was, to close those channels. It is also of interest to consider the validity of this analysis. Against those who contended that the stock market was absorbing an ever-growing share of the available credit, the opposite school argued that it was not absorbing any credit at all. If certain persons borrowed money to buy stock at higher prices, they must have been matched by others who were realizing stock and, if the latter used the proceeds to buy more stock, still others would be in receipt of money and that money would be available for industrial or commercial expansion. In fact there would be no net absorption of credit, since loans raised for stock-market speculation passed through the stock market like a sieve and came out on the other side where they were available for normal industrial purposes. A mass of literature was composed at the time on the subject of this debate, and I confess that I did not find it enlightening or feel convinced that either side decisively established its case. In this matter, as in so many others, Keynes' subsequent analysis provided a completely satisfying answer. In a general way loans do pass through the stock market as through a sieve, and would only fail to do so to the precise extent that some speculators were building up a bear position, viz. beginning to hold cash in excess of their normal requirements because they deemed it dangerous any longer to have their capital, or all of it, in securities at their existing price level. In fact, it is not the wild and giddy speculators who deprive industry of money, but the cool wise heads as and when they begin to take precautions against an impending stock-market slump. I believe that this analysis is correct and will explain the phenomena of 1929. It also indicates that the sectional approach to the problem referred to above was not likely to succeed.

Beyond the controversy as to whether the Federal Reserve System should have done something that it did not do prior to October 1929, there is the further controversy as to whether it should have done more than it did subsequently to restore the situation by making money very easy. Actually, after the crash, it reversed engines with remarkable speed and efficiency. In two months its open market holdings of U.S. securities rose from $154 million to $446 million. There was a further gradual rise thereafter. This reflationary effort is of comparable order of magnitude to what was done during the recessions of 1924 and 1927. But was this sufficient? The reverse that had now occurred was clearly of larger magnitude than earlier setbacks. Professor Hawtrey has urged that the operations should have been on a greater scale and that the reduction in interest rates, which the System had by now got into the habit of regarding as secondary to open market contraction, should have been speedier. I was heart and soul with him. For some years all those interested in monetary matters had been watching this brave experiment in thermostatic control by the Federal Reserve System closely. Now it seemed that the testing time had come. A larger reverse had occurred and bolder operations were called for. Would the System be true to its principles? Much seemed to depend on this, and did depend on it. If the System failed at this juncture to preserve monetary stability, doubt would be thrown on the doctrine of the reformers that monetary policy could play a dominant part in ironing out the trade cycle. The matter is a little more complicated. If the System did not adopt bold measures, the sceptics would regard this as confirming their views, but reformers would be able to argue that they were in the right, since, they would say, the depression had grown not because monetary policy was powerless to prevent it, but because the monetary authorities had not taken appropriate action. But they would be on difficult ground, because a purely hypothetical claim does not carry conviction; and so it all turned out. The monetary school, not merely in the United States, but throughout the world, was greatly weakened, and the majority view came to be that the monetary weapon was not potent enough to save the world from depressions.

An event of first importance occurred in the spring of 1930. The Open Market Committee was reconstituted and made to comprise one member from each of the twelve Federal Reserve Banks. This naturally altered the balance of power in that body. The reconstitution may be regarded as a normal extension of the democratic principle and the removal of an anomaly. To-day we have not yet reached the end of the tendency in world affairs by which a copy-book interpretation of the democratic principle has to be applied in ever-widening spheres, regardless of whether it is appropriate or serves the true purposes of democracy. The Federal Reserve Board had proposed this reform some time earlier, and it has been suggested that this move reflected its desire to shift power away from New York somewhat. Beyond all this there was a deeper reason. The fact that a reconstitution that had been on the agenda for some time was carried out in the spring of 1930 was, of course, not disconnected with the antecedent crash and the deep disturbance to men's minds and the suspicions engendered by it. This reconstitution should be regarded as a belated manifestation of that old, old prejudice against Eastern domination. It was Andrew Jackson striking his last blow.

I had luncheon in the offices of the Federal Reserve Bank of New York in August 1930. I was a youthful enthusiast, green and callow no doubt, urging with all the force at my command the Hawtrey doctrine. I named a figure of $1000 million as an appropriate purchase of U.S. securities over and above what had so far been done. I urged what Keynes was already saying in England that, if the slump was allowed to gather further momentum, it was likely to bring in its wake something worse than monetary bankruptcy, namely, political upheaval and social revolution. I was surprised at the attention paid by the top-ranking officials of the Bank to one so young. They raised various objections of the usual kind. But before the interview was over, they had come clean. They agreed with me ; what I said was precisely what they wanted to do ; but they could not do it, because they could not secure agreement from the banks of the interior. The reconstitution of the Open Market Committee had caused a shift of power, and the Bank of New York was no longer able to collect enough support to carry the day in the Committee.

The scene was engraved on my mind by the last words of my host. I was in the United States at the time on a Library Commission appointed by Oxford University. I was considerably junior to all and very much junior indeed to all but one of my colleagues, and vastly inferior to them all in academic renown. I found that I attached much more importance than they did to open access to the bookshelves for research workers, and feared that I might have to write a minority report over my own name alone. I mentioned these matters in small talk at the luncheon table, deeming these bankers safely far removed from those who had cognizance of my mission. As I departed, my host extended his hand. 'Well,' he said, 'I hope that you may have more success in persuading your conservative colleagues of the value of open shelf-access, than we have had in persuading the banks of the interior of the value of an extension of Open Market purchases at this time.'

The purchases were not made. Such an experiment was carried out in the summer of 1932, when 1100 million dollars worth of U.S. securities were purchased in the course of eleven weeks. But by then the situation had degenerated out of recognition, and it could not be hoped that the experiment would have the success that it might have had two years earlier. Would the monetary weapon have indeed been strong enough to counteract the depressive forces of that time? If the Federal Reserve System had in the summer of 1930 purchased 1000 million dollars worth of securities, or, maybe, 2000 million dollars worth — these sums are not large in comparison with subsequent developments — would this have prevented the progressive deterioration in the United States during the following years? Had it done that, it would thereby have prevented the progressive deterioration in the world as a whole, would have prevented also the rise of the Nazis to power and the Second World War. But would it indeed have prevented the progressive deterioration in the United States? I am not so confident now as I was then.

Thereafter the scene shifted. The hopes that were built on wise Federal Reserve management in the 'twenties were belied. But it must be added that the havoc wrought by the slump would undoubtedly have been worse had the Federal Reserve System not been in existence, providing easy credit from its large reserves and taking all reasonable measures to relieve the situation, short of the supreme experiment. During the New Deal period, while there were a number of interesting developments, central reserve policy was less important in the total picture. Since the main objective was to restimulate the economy into greater activity, very easy credit conditions were maintained in the United States, as they were in England, fairly continuously for the rest of the inter-war period.

At this point mention must be made of Roosevelt's devaluation of the dollar in 1933. This was presented as an attempt to raise prices in the United States, as these were too low for business to be profitable. But the idea that they could be raised to a higher level by raising the dollar price of gold seemed to rest on a very crude theory of money. Nevertheless, looking back on that event and recognizing that it did not secure and could not have secured the result postulated, I am bound to say that I judge that it was on the whole beneficial. I am conscious that this is a very unpopular view in certain quarters, and for that reason I venture to mention an episode which, I feel, entitles me to speak with freedom and a clear conscience. In the autumn of 1933 I wrote a letter to President Roosevelt, which I induced a number of fellow economists to sign after having amended its wording to suit them. This letter reached the President's hands through the intervention of a friend and we received word that he had discussed its content with his circle of advisers.[1] The letter, which touched on various aspects of New Deal policy, advised firmly against the gold revaluation policy. The case was argued fairly fully that it could not attain the end desired and would only serve to increase the embarrassment of those countries that were still adhering to their pre-slump gold parities.

All this may have been true, and yet it may also be true that the gold policy was helpful to the outside world; and, even if it had no appreciable effect on the United States economy directly, it may have benefited the United States indirectly to the extent that it aided world recovery by raising the commodity value of gold.

[1] This episode occurred nearly a year earlier than the President's much-bruited interview with Keynes.

This was the opposite of what was intended, which was to reduce the commodity value of the dollar. The increase in the dollar price raised world liquidity and enabled nations striving to recover to pursue a more liberal policy than they could otherwise have done. The low commodity value of available gold stocks had been a constant source of embarrassment in the 'twenties; Roosevelt's action eased the situation in this regard in the 'thirties, and while in that post-slump period many new restrictions were imposed on world trade, we must surely judge that the restrictions would have been much more severe, had the gold situation not been rendered so much easier. Of course it is quite wrong to argue that Roosevelt in any sense debauched the dollar; its great appreciation in terms of commodities between 1929 and 1933 was an evil; the devaluation had little immediate effect on its commodity value, and by 1939 prices had only climbed back three-eighths of the way up the hill that they had descended prior to it. Thus the dollar was still worth, when the Second War broke out, about one-third more than it had been in 1929. I am convinced that another rise in the dollar price of gold is a necessary prerequisite for any large movement towards more liberal conditions in international trade to-day.

After a period of experiment, the gold value of the dollar was refixed in January 1934. Apart from the devaluation, the Gold Reserve Act of that date contained a provision of most far-reaching significance, the consequences of which are not yet fully unfolded. It was laid down that the dollar was no longer to be convertible into gold for individuals, but only for foreign central banks or monetary authorities. This meant that the United States was abandoning the gold standard as that had always hitherto been understood. It would be a foolish man who supposed that he could summarize the remote consequences of such a breach with a system that had prevailed for centuries in the civilized world.

The effect of this measure was nul until the outbreak of the Second World War. This was due to the operation of the free market for gold bullion in London. There any individual holder of the dollar could obtain gold at the official United States valuation via sterling, the sterling price of gold bullion being governed in that period by the dollar shipping parity. It would not be an exaggeration to say that we in Britain maintained the United States gold standard for them during this period.

The war brought the free bullion market in London to an end. Thereafter a premium on gold against the dollar developed, and has been very high in certain post-war years. For a time the International Monetary Fund frowned upon the sales of newly mined gold direct to the free markets, but later relaxed its attitude. The free markets then received gold in large quantities and the premium has accordingly been reduced to a low level, but only at the price of the loss of much newly mined gold from the monetary circulation.

One of the main objectives of strict adherence to convertibility has historically been to discourage private hoardings of the precious metals. It was argued correctly that if the individual was educated by a slow process to regard paper as being as good as metal, simply because it was freely convertible into metal at any time without let or hindrance or inquisition, he would be weaned from the desire to hold precious metal. This slow process of education had had a considerable measure of success. There was bound to be a reverse when the various paper currencies of the world lost value during the Second World War. The revived tendency to hoard was officially encouraged for short-period reasons connected with the war, which were sound ; the precious metal was despatched to countries of the Near

East and Far East in the hope that they would substitute gold hoarding for commodity hoarding which was detrimental to the war effort. There can be no doubt that the inconvertibility of the dollar has aggravated this tendency since the war at a time when there is all too little of the yellow metal to satisfy monetary requirements.

I accordingly find myself in sympathy with those who have recently been advocating a restoration of the gold standard in the United States. I am told that these advocates are in many cases persons of very conservative opinions with which I would not be likely to agree. It is possible, however, to hold erroneous opinions about a number of matters and yet to hold a sound opinion about an all-important one. I judge that it would be of great benefit if the United States restored the convertibility of the dollar. I would only add that, as a preliminary to doing so, it would be needful to alter the present gold valuation of the dollar.

One or two of the changes that occurred in the 'thirties are worthy of mention. We need not take time with various measures for liberalizing the lending powers of the System, which were designed to enable it to give the maximum assistance during the stresses of the slump. Of far-reaching importance was the Securities Exchange Act of June 6, 1934. By it the Federal Reserve Board was given power to regulate stock brokers' margins. This was clearly directly relevant to the dilemma presented prior to the crash of October 1929, which was discussed above. It has remained an important weapon in the armoury of central monetary control, and has been used from time to time. There was a period of a year after the Second World War when the requirement for purchasers of stock was raised to 100 per cent.

Another interesting power was given in the famous Thomas amendment of 1933; this power was a sop to disciplinarians in an otherwise inflationary measure. The Federal Reserve Board was allowed to raise the percentage of reserves required to be held by member banks in the times of emergency. This matter was regularized and generalized in the Banking Act of 1935; the Board was allowed to raise statutory requirements to a maximum level of not more than double. This gave it another important weapon of credit control, which has been used. It may be regarded as an alternative to the open market sales of U.S. securities, and it was considered valuable to have this alternative at a time when the Federal Government was tending towards a deficit position and it might be awkward to have a disturbance of security values. It could be objected that if an increase of legal reserve requirements compelled member banks to sell, this too would create a disturbance; but in certain technical situations it might be convenient to have the choice between these two ways of enforcing restriction.

During this period, a phenomenon developed which was without precedent in American banking history. Many member banks began to hold reserves in excess of their legal requirements. It would have been highly beneficial had the great banks of New York adopted this habit in the half century before 1914. But the Americans tended to take the natural and enterprising view that money was there to be used. The new-found tendency in the 'thirties was due to a number of large forces operating in the same direction. Trade was in the depths of the depression and easy-credit conditions did not bring customers in to borrow. At the same time, there was a huge inflow of gold to the United States, partly to cover her normal trading surpluses, but in greater part to cover a massive outflow of capital from insecure and frightened Europe. This gold automatically enlarged the reserves of the member banks. The Federal Government, perhaps to ease the sense of guilt arising from running deficits in peace-time, was tending to borrow at long term. Thus the member banks had a plethora of reserves and a shortage of short-term demand for them. The dead condition of the stock market, together with the Securities Exchange Act, restricted the demand for brokers' loans. Each bank naturally felt chary of piling up too large an investment in long-dated governments. Thus there was nothing for it but to let the excess reserves stand. The Board could, indeed, have eliminated much of this excess position by a heroic sale of its own Government Securities; but this would not have been popular with the Treasury when the government was a net borrower; furthermore, the System was prepared as part of its policy to acquiesce in excess reserves outstanding; that was easy money with a vengeance.

Under its new-found power the System could also eliminate much of the excess reserves by raising legal reserve requirements, and this was done in 1936, when it was judged that a little damping down was needed, or, perhaps one should rather say, as a preparatory measure, to put the System in a position where it could execute a real contraction, should conditions seem to be becoming inflationary. At the same time the incoming gold was sterilized by being acquired by the Treasury against long-dated securities sold in the market. These slightly restrictive measures were not maintained for long; 1937 saw the onset of a new recession of some severity, and engines were accordingly reversed.

Mention must also be made of the Federal Deposit Insurance Corporation, established by the Bank Act of 1935, to take the place of an interim post-crash arrangement. A plan of this kind was much discussed, with Democratic backing, in the years when the Federal Reserve System was being planned, but it was then considered unsound and not adopted. For the rest, the Bank Act of 1935 was centralizing in tendency.

One other gadget may, by a forward glance, be mentioned here; in some ways, it was the most interesting of them all. In pursuance of legislation in 1941 the Federal Reserve System issued its regulation W, by which it prescribed conditions for the hire-purchase of consumer durables. If and as we return to normal peace-time conditions, the relaxation or restriction of credit terms under regulation W might be a most potent instrument for ironing out the trade cycle. The consumption of soft goods proceeds fairly regularly through years of good and bad trade, always provided that fluctuations in employment itself are not excessive. The consumer has much elbow-room in the timing of the purchases of durables, and therewith the power to set up a vicious circle of expansion or contraction. Congress, which has now come to regard the Federal Reserve System, along with its traditional banking powers, as part of the normal order of established things, is not quite sure that it has not gone too far in giving it the power to regulate hire-purchase terms; this involves allowing it to enter rather intimately into the affairs of the citizen. In the post-war period it has shown an oscillation of policy, agreeing to and withdrawing this power by fits and starts.

The period of the Second World War may be characterized very briefly. In the United States, as in the United Kingdom, the governmental borrowing that was necessary was executed on extraordinarily cheap terms. This is in notable contrast with the First World War. In the case of both countries, the second war imposed a much heavier economic strain than the first, and lasted longer; in both countries it was financed by cheap, instead of by expensive, borrowing; and in both countries the amount of inflation arising during the war was far less. This remarkable achievement must, in fairness, be attributed to the thinking of the late Lord Keynes. In Britain his influence was direct; in the United States his name has been unpopular for a number of reasons, many of them erroneous, and the idea that he was responsible for the low cost of the war in terms of interest charges might be resented; yet it can hardly be denied that it was the effect of the absorption of his thought by the U.S. Treasury authorities. For indeed this thought embodies a great paradox. By orthodox notions it would seem that, if borrowing on a vast scale is to be undertaken, far beyond anything that has even been dreamt of in peace-time, a somewhat higher price must be paid to the lender. This would seem reasonable on theory; it is also endorsed by the universal experience of past history. Keynes argued on the basis of his own very special theory concerning the rate of interest that all this was quite unnecessary, that the rate of interest was not indeed determined by the balance of the demand and supply of loans — and therefore need not be pushed up by a great increase of borrowing — but was determined by the balance in the demand and supply of liquidity. These doctrines were put into operation in both countries with complete success; their success appears to confirm the Keynes theory. Nor did inflationary consequences follow from all the cheap borrowing.

Thus the war finance was conducted with marked, and indeed outstanding, success. All the more disappointing was it that a period of strong inflation followed the cessation of hostilities. This was in contrast to the aftermath of the First World War, when the inflationary period was terminated in little more than a year. The position was disappointing in Britain, but still more so in the United States, as may be seen from the following table.

It is really pathetic that the price level in the United States should have risen substantially more in three short years of peace than in six years of preparation and conduct for war. The inflationary pressures continued to be strong in both countries, owing to the needs of reconstruction. It is probable that the pressure in Britain was considerably more intense owing to the need for a vast expansion in her exports over the pre-war level. The United States also executed a comparable expansion of exports, but in her case the proportion of total resources going into this activity is so much smaller that the increase of exports which she executed imposed far less strain.

	U.S.	U.K.
General Prices —	%	%
1939–45	+38	+66
1945–8	+50	+30
1939–48	+107	+116
Wages Rates —	%	%
1939–45	+57	+50
1945–8	+33	+23
1939–48	+110	+84

In both countries there were the same kind of arguments and reasons for continuing the cheap money policy. One was the size of the National Debt: in the United States it was the equivalent of somewhat over one year's national income, and in Britain of about three years' national income; any rise in service charges would impose a burden upon the taxpayer. In both countries some thought was given to the danger of a post-war slump, and the need for having low interest rates established, should one supervene. Once the rates on long-term bonds rose substantially, it might not be too easy to re-establish low rates; it had proved difficult after the First World War.

Then why not treat the post-war period as one had treated the war period? If one had got through the terrific strain of the war with easy money and small inflation, should one not be able to get through the much smaller strain of post-war reconstruction without inflation? But in fact there was a big difference. For an essential part of the war-time pattern was the whole panoply of control, and in the United States at least citizens were not willing to endure this for much longer. Here we get a difference between the two countries. The United States controls were, in the main, abandoned in 1946, while the essential British controls were sustained for a much longer period. Britain should thus have been able to hold inflation more sharply in check than the United States, and she did so; her failure to get rid of it completely was due to the fact that, although the controls existed, the authorities were not willing to use them to repress the expenditure on capital account to the level that would have been needed, if inflation was to be avoided altogether.

There was another difference between the two countries. Britain's attempt to maintain the long rate of interest at around $2\frac{1}{2}$ per cent. broke down during the crisis of the winter of 1946–7, and thereafter the rate went steadily upwards. In the United States, the rate on long-dated bonds was kept at $2\frac{1}{2}$ per cent. for more than six years.

Thus the broad picture is that both countries had more inflation than one might have thought tolerable in peace-time. Britain was under severer over-all pressure, but maintained controls for longer, and after a year and a half allowed the long-term rate of interest to rise. The United States was under less pressure, but abandoned controls and maintained cheap money in the fullest sense. The net effect was that she suffered from a more severe inflation than Britain.[1] While Britain was having to

[1] I take my comparison to the year 1948, because thereafter the position was to be bedevilled by the devaluation of sterling. The rise of prices that occurred in Britain subsequently was the inevitable effect of the devaluation, and has nothing whatever to do with the forces discussed in the text above.

surrender on the long-term interest front, the United
States authorities were struggling with an opposite difficulty, namely trying to prevent the bond rate falling
too far below $2\frac{1}{2}$ per cent.! This tendency, it must
hastily be said, was in no wise due to the natural forces
of the market, but was the effect of a rather rigid policy
of maintaining the rate on 90-day bills at $\frac{3}{8}$ of 1 per cent.
This policy involved monetary expansion and put press-
ure upon the member banks to move towards longer-
dated securities; hence the tendency of the bond rate to
fall still further. It was nearly a year after the British
gave up the unequal struggle of the bond rate that the
American authorities decided to allow the 90-day bill
rate to rise. Thereafter, there was no tendency for the
bond rate to fall much below $2\frac{1}{2}$ per cent., and at times
the bond market had to be strongly supported by the
Federal Reserve System to prevent a rise. In discussions
on this topic, we find much reference to the need to
maintain an 'orderly' market. Apparently the idea was
that if the rate was allowed to move too far from that
$2\frac{1}{2}$ per cent., to which business men had become accustomed as something endorsed by the authorities, there
might be a horrid collapse, involving a wide movement
in the rates towards the more old-fashioned norms and
entailing a collapse of capital values that was capable of
ruining many member banks. There may well have been
something in this idea of an 'orderly' bond market.

But if we stand back and regard this post-war period
in broad perspective, we may be a little puzzled. What
was expected to happen? The British position was
clear; the authorities were determined to maintain
controls. If there is undue inflationary pressure simply
arising from the needs of reconstruction, if all controls
are removed and if the supply of money is governed
entirely by the principle that as much money will be
supplied as is needed to maintain a $2\frac{1}{2}$ per cent. bond
rate, what is there to prevent an all-out inflation?

Everything will depend on how quickly prices and wages chase each other upwards. It may be argued that, while there was a continued spiralling in the United States and this was acquiesced in, yet, if the chase had become too fast and furious, the bond market policy would have been abandoned and the Federal Reserve would have come in with all its immense powers to secure a disinflation. Nevertheless, it remains somewhat unsatisfactory that a rise in general prices of as much as 50 per cent. in three war years was allowed. It may be that in the first year after the war the thinking of the authorities was governed by the idea that they, like the British, would keep the controls in being until the worst dangers were over. Congress did not allow that. There followed a period of somewhat confused *laissez-faire*.

This is not quite the end of our story. Inflationary pressures terminated in 1948, and there was a moderate recession, commonly diagnosed as an inventory recession, in 1949. The post-war problem seemed to be at an end. Happily, the recession was not severe and a recovery was staged. But then came a new complication — the Korean outbreak. During the earlier period, there had been rumours of lack of accord between the Federal Reserve authorities and the Treasury. It is not to be supposed that the Federal Reserve was pressing for an all-out policy of disinflation, such as in retrospect one might deem desirable. But there were questions of degree; the Federal Reserve was restive under the insistence on a rigidly fixed 90-day bill rate, and an almost fixed bond rate, which might be deemed to transform U.S. bonds into money. There were murmurings and potentialities of serious trouble; the Korean War brought this matter to a head. A rapid inflation was quickly brought on by consumer and other stock-pilings in the period after the outbreak, and a vast rearmament programme was under way. There was a serious danger of really drastic inflation. What about this $2\frac{1}{2}$ per cent. bond rate? Would it, indeed, be regarded as sacrosanct through thick and thin? There was discord, followed by accord. In March 1951, at long last, the rigid system was ended by agreement, and it may be deemed that once again the Federal Reserve System has authority to conduct bond market operations in a way to secure steady credit conditions. It would be difficult for it to push this power *à outrance*; but within discretionary limits it may regard itself as free to act. A curious interlude is now over, and we have the Federal Reserve System with us again in something like its old shape.

III

TOWARDS INTERNATIONAL
CO-OPERATION

In the preceding lectures I have been regarding the dollar as it has appeared to the Americans who invented it for use, and are in fact its main users; the time has come when we must change our point of view and survey it as it appears to the outside world.

Considered as a domestic product, the dollar has had a tempestuous history. Hamilton and his colleagues had to cater for the needs of people who had become accustomed to lax issues and inflationary tendencies. During the colonial period, London had indeed made repeated attempts to enforce discipline; her efforts had been insufficient to secure good order, but much too great for her own popularity. Indeed it has been suggested that, if we look below the surface, we shall find the true cause that precipitated revolt to lie, not so much in a few trumpery taxes, which doubtless made a good political issue, as in the British opposition, reaffirmed by the notorious Grenville in 1763, to inflationary issues. That was where the rub was really felt.

Such being the early history, it was not to be expected that inflationary bouts would be altogether avoided; but from the time of Hamilton onwards, strong attempts were made to hold the line. The forces of expansion and the forces of discipline were kept in equipoise. The dollar survived the various storms remarkably well; lapses were followed by restorations, and there has been no break in continuity. If order was not always maintained, expansionist episodes may have played a helpful part in the mighty economic tasks that have been achieved with such marvellous celerity.

At long last in 1914 the United States came into line with the usage of other mature countries by accepting a central banking arrangement in the form of the Federal Reserve System. In the 'twenties the highest hopes were attached, both at home and abroad, to the somewhat unorthodox essays in monetary management undertaken by the System. It seemed that she had assumed world leadership in applying the most modern ideas to currency and credit regulation. Unhappily, hopes were dashed by the events of 1929. There followed a longish interlude in which less emphasis was placed on the power and importance of monetary management. The reaction was too great. Informed opinion swung from the view that monetary policy could cure the trade cycle to the view that it was of quite minor importance. This reaction was not peculiar to the United States, but world-wide. There has since been a counter-reaction, and it may be hoped that a balanced view now prevails; monetary management should not be regarded as a panacea, but it has its important part to play.

After the war there was some anxiety that the Federal Reserve System had lost too much power to the Treasury as custodian of the interest that the public has in the economic servicing of the National Debt. This anxiety has been largely relieved by the accord of March 1951.

It is now perhaps not too much to hope that the System will have power enough to curb further inflation in all circumstances short of war or rearmament plans greater than those yet known. The possibility of depression presents a more serious problem. Here, too, there are grounds for hope. Some foreign observers fear that the sentiment favourable to *laissez-faire* in the United States will constitute an insuperable obstacle to adequate curative measures. They probably do not make enough allowance for the wide gulf that now exists between inner opinion and platform opinion — a curious and rather uncomfortable characteristic of developed democracy, which may constitute Nature's make-weight to the extreme application of formal democratic principles. Thus on the whole we may deem that there are very fair chances of a good internal management of the dollar, which may set an example to the world.

To the Americans recently, especially in the post-war years, the dollar has seemed faulty in being rather considerably too elastic. To the outside world, on the contrary, it has presented itself as having a rock-like hardness. This technical quality, which it has undoubtedly had in foreign exchange markets, has become merged in the imaginations of men with the awe inspired by the spectacle of the great economic pre-eminence of the United States. Someone invented the expression, the 'Almighty Dollar'.

There is a double justification for including a treatment of its external aspect in a history of the dollar. First, the large and growing relative importance of American trade, and the influence of American demand for goods upon the world price structure, cause the evolution of the dollar to play a part in the history of most other countries. Their economic annals cannot be adequately recorded without reference to the dollar, and their hopes and fears for the future are much influenced by expectations in regard to it. The history of the dollar is now an integral part of world history. Secondly, to look at the matter more formally, the dollar has by a vote of Congress acquired certain new characteristics through American membership of the International Monetary Fund. There are certain rights and duties connected with that membership that are now constitutionally just as much part of the definition of the dollar as the body of laws relating to minting, note

issue and banking. Thus formally, as well as practi-
cally, the future of the dollar can depend to some extent
on what other people think and do in relation to it. It
is expedient therefore to take a brief retrospect of their
views upon this matter.

Prior to 1914 events in dollar history, such as the
rise and fall of greenbacks, may have been observed
with much interest, but were not felt to be of close
domestic concern to other nations. (I make an exception,
however, for the silver agitation.) During the First
World War, the dollar question came nearer home,
partly owing to the great debts to the United States
incurred by the allies, and partly owing to the drain of
gold thither. It is with the latter that we shall now be
concerned. Between the end of 1914 and the end of
1918, the U.S. gold stock rose from $1800 million to
$3160 million. This phenomenon was observed with
some anxiety; but it was not in the least degree unnatural or surprising; it was perfectly plain why such
a drain towards the great supplier occurred in the circumstances of the First World War. A similar drain
occurred in the Second World War. After the end of
1918 there was an interlude lasting for two years. But
then, after the onset of the post-war slump, a new drain
began; between the end of 1920 and the end of 1922
the United States gold stock rose from $2926 million to
$4499 million.[1] This gave more serious grounds for
alarm. It was understood that the United States had
assumed a greater economic importance in the world
scene. In the old days London had been a magnet for
gold; but she had a mechanism, already described, by
which gold was no sooner attracted than repelled. Gold
might proceed from all parts to the London bullion
market, but it came out again, so that there was little
net absorption or strain upon the liquidity position of

[1] Figures relating to gold stocks are derived from the Annual Reports
of the Federal Reserve Board.

other countries. Now here was a new kind of monster; it attracted gold — the old London monster did that. The new monster had a new kind of characteristic; it not only attracted gold, but seemed capable of holding and absorbing it. The basic reasons for this were given in the foregoing lecture. It must be repeated with emphasis that no blame is to be attached for this new kind of behaviour; nor is it to be supposed that it was on balance detrimental to world interests. It was said at the time, and has often been said since, that the United States did not play the rules of the gold standard game. This is quite a fair statement. It does not follow that she ought to have played that game according to the established rules. Had the Federal Reserve System expanded credit and currency in full proportion to the gold inflow, that must have generated a vast inflation, and it can by no means be held that such a course of conduct would have been more beneficial to the outside world than what actually happened, a prudent, steadying control of the internal credit structure. The fact that Britain almost automatically re-lent abroad the gold that came in while the United States did not, is connected with the basic characteristics and past history of the two economies. It would have been foolish and ignorant to prescribe to New York the old London rules.

The fact remains, however, that this new kind of behaviour by the New York monster was likely, if it persisted, to make a big difference to everything. The whole position needed thinking out anew. Policy requires some understanding, if only in rough outline, of how the economic mechanism works. Text-books on foreign exchanges gave an account, which may have corresponded to reality reasonably well. To the extent that their authors were not writing purely abstract theories about worlds unrealized, but had their feet on the ground, they derived their realistic touch by an observation of how the London markets worked. They may have been at fault in implying that the way things worked out there would necessarily be the way things would always work out within any group of gold standard nations. They obtained their data from London and then generalized them as applicable to any world of gold standard countries considered in the abstract. It is a remarkable example of Keynes' penetration and vision that he pointed this out as early as 1912,[1] before the great disturbance caused by the First World War. It is to be feared that there are some people whose thinking is still pre-1912. The whole subject was not re-thought out in the 'twenties. New maxims appropriate to a different mode of working of the gold standard were not formulated. This was due in part to the unhappy fact that the human intellect has not so far shown itself well-qualified for such a task; and that holds true to-day. It has had great triumphs in dissecting the atomic nucleus, but money has, on the whole, been too difficult a subject for it. What it has done sufficiently well has been to analyse any system that is already in working order; systems of incredible delicacy and subtlety have grown up by trial and error under the pressure of practical exigencies. To work out in advance and in the abstract what may be required by a radically changed situation is a more formidable and baffling task.

But there was another reason why the re-thinking was not done. It proved after all that there was for the time being no urgent need for it. The gold drain ceased at the end of 1924, and in the following decade the United States was not a net absorber. The events of 1920–24 could easily be rationalized. The United States was the only important gold standard country, and the peculiar phenomenon of absorption might be attributed to that — indeed was so attributed in the classic Tenth Report already cited. When the other

[1] *Indian Currency and Finance.*

countries returned to the gold standard, the drain ceased. That was that.

The proximate cause of the cessation of the drain was that the United States became a large-scale foreign investor. This balanced her favourable position on current account. Those who insisted on being anxious and on taking a gloomy view, diverted their attention to the quality of the United States lending. While it was considered quite right in the abstract that she should lend, there were fears that the lending was not altogether wise. In the offering of foreign bonds to American buyers, there was too much of the atmosphere of the bucket-shop, or even of the tout who takes domestic appliances from door to door. One should not, however, be unduly captious; it was good that the United States was looking outwards; there is every reason to suppose that, had other circumstances remained favourable, a better selection of investment opportunities would in due course have been made and sounder methods of flotation adopted.

A graver reason for anxiety occurred in due course. During 1929 there was a sharp drop in foreign lending. In the years 1924 to 1929 net long-term lending had averaged $776 million, with $847 million in 1928; in 1929 this dropped to $278 million. To take another set of figures, the foreign securities publicly offered in the U.S. market averaged $1148 million, with $1484 million in 1928, but in 1929 they were only $696 million. This drop was not the consequence of the Wall Street crash, but of the Wall Street boom; U.S. money (as well as foreign money) was attracted by the whirligig there. Why invest abroad, when such huge profits could be made at home? This sharp decline of lending created disturbance outside. The point may not be of great lasting interest, since it is hoped that, owing to the Securities Exchange Act and other devices, a Wall Street boom of the 1929 character will never recur. The episode is worth mentioning as one factor that built up anxiety abroad about having too intimate a relation with an economy that was capable of such violent oscillation. Some now hope that the United States, after largely keeping out of the foreign investment business for a quarter of a century, may resume foreign investment on a substantial scale. While there is a good deal of fallacy in those who advocate this as a method for securing equilibrium in the world balance of payments, it would be desirable for the United States, to the extent that she has a surplus of saving, to make this available in under-developed regions that are sorely in need of capital. If such investment assumed large dimensions, it would be important to have some kind of assurance that the tap would not be suddenly turned off, as it was in 1929. The sudden reduction of that year, even if exonerated from being a leading cause of the world slump, may have done harm by creating initial conditions in Europe that made quick recovery more difficult. It must be admitted that there is no easy way of obtaining an assurance in advance against a sudden down-turn in lending; many light-headed things have been said about this. The fact that the problem is difficult does not entitle us to dismiss it from our minds.

The slump itself was a more important matter. Foreign opinion cannot rid itself of the view that the main causes of this unparalleled disaster lay in the United States. This still seems to be the reasonable opinion. The external manifestation was a continuing fall in the amount of dollars spent on foreign goods and services from $6973 million in 1929 to $2405 million in 1932. This involved rather a severe shock.

If the allegation of American responsibility is correct, it does not follow that we must expect a recurrence. This question of impending American slumps has become something of an obsession with the outside world. It is sometimes forgotten that Americans no less, nay more, than others suffered from the reverse, and that they are likely to make manful efforts to prevent another disorder of that sort; nor is it characteristic of the Americans to make a resolve and then fail to put it into effect. The notion that it would be wise to limit economic relations with the United States because they are likely to have a series of great slumps in the future seems wrong-headed and even rather fatuous. It may sometimes be worse — a mere pretext for what is desired on other grounds.

Unhappily for the development of this obsession, the United States, not content with having had a mighty slump in 1929–33, and barely recovering from it, had another slump, which by all standards except American would be regarded as one of great magnitude, in 1937–8. Dollars spent on the purchase of foreign goods and services fell from $4603 million in 1937 to $3250 million in 1938; a decline not far short of one-third is no laughing matter. These fears have an abiding influence to the present day. They were prominent in the war-time discussions of the problem, which we shall consider shortly.

In 1934, when the American economy was still in the doldrums, the drain of gold began again. In the five-year period 1934–8 the average annual movement of gold to the United States was no less than $1395 million. This has given rise to important misconceptions. It has repeatedly been argued that the United States in this period maintained an oppressively creditor position. Actually her surplus on trading account could have been paid for by less than a quarter of this amount of gold, and, when her deficit on account of invisible services is brought in, it appears that less than one-fifth was needed to pay for the current U.S. surplus. By far the greater part of the gold flow represented a flight of capital. Exaggerated notions under this head had an important influence on opinion.

It may be expedient to dwell briefly on this capital

flow. From the point of view of the world balance it was a perverse phenomenon. The United States is not short of capital; rather it is the rest of the world that is relatively short. The flow had two main reasons. The outside world took a more balanced and phlegmatic view of the prospects of the American economy than the Americans themselves, who had become unduly cast down by the ravages of the depression; and it assessed the probable yield of investments in the United States as good. More important was the fear of war.

During the Second World War, it became a fixed point of doctrine in British circles that it would not be possible to permit an unimpeded outflow of capital after the war. Even in the piping times of peace a drain of gold to the United States on the scale of 1934–8 could not have been long sustained. It was intolerable that the world's liquid resources should be sucked away, with all the consequent embarrassments, by this perverse movement of capital. How much worse would it be, when Britain would have in addition to sustain the vast additional burdens expected to fall on her shoulders as the aftermath of war. The question may be raised whether it was reasonable to expect the flow of capital to continue after the war, since the special causes afore-mentioned might not then be operating. If the flow was unlikely to occur, then it would be unnecessary to legislate against it, and, if unnecessary, undesirable, since such legislation was bound to have troublesome implications.

In British circles Keynes acquired considerable influence in the course of the war, and he favoured the control of capital movements for more general reasons. It was a thesis that he had been expounding for some twenty years, that the outflow of capital from Britain, if unimpeded, might be excessive. He held that if massive unemployment was to be prevented in Britain, it would be needful for industry at home to obtain long-term capital on cheap terms. He feared that if the outflow of capital was unimpeded, the competition of the demand for capital in other parts of the world would make the price at which capital was offered to home industry too expensive, and that a deflationary process would be set up. Furthermore, he feared lest, in order to generate a foreign trade surplus sufficient to cover such an outflow of capital, a deflation would be needed to curtail imports to the necessary level. These views were not in accord with traditional economic doctrine. Keynes spent many years in vindicating them by elaborate arguments that touch the very foundations of economic theory. This is not the place to elaborate them. I would only give a pointer to those not learned in economics, who may have heard of a Keynesian revolution, but have not the faintest idea what it is all about. His essential difference with the older theorists is intimately connected with the point that the unimpeded flow of capital among the nations will not necessarily secure the best distribution of it for each and all and full employment everywhere. The fact that Keynes had this reason, which may almost be called an esoteric one, for wishing to regulate the outflow of capital, had influence. The doctrine that the movement of capital may have to be controlled from time to time became strongly held as a principle of official British policy, was accepted by the Americans, and is embodied in the Articles of Agreement of the International Monetary Fund.

In the event the movement of capital has been controlled since the war, and there have been good reasons for that, but not precisely the reasons that were foreseen at the time. The fear of a third World War has played the same part more recently as the fear of a second World War played in the 'thirties. So long as that fear subsists, even in slight degree, no sensible person will propose the abrogation of control over capital movements. Secondly, it is the consequence of political trends in Europe that the rights of property are deemed to be somewhat less secure there than they are in the United States. This gives a political motive for moving across, quite apart from normal economic incentives, and it is to be feared that this motive may remain for some time.

It is still not clear how far it is possible to reconcile a fairly strict control over capital movements with those greater commercial freedoms that have been the aim of American and British policy in recent years, and with currency convertibility in anything approaching the older sense of that term. It is not easy to control capital movement. But the need appears imperative. This is a vexing problem that must remain in the background of our thoughts upon all those matters that I am about to relate.

After the slump the United States maintained the convertibility of the dollar *vis-à-vis* foreign central banks and monetary authorities, but not for individuals. Meanwhile two new types of monetary system were developing elsewhere. The British were compelled to abandon the convertibility of sterling under pressure of events in 1931, and the pound became a purely paper currency. It was, however, freely marketable. No restrictions were put upon the holders of sterling who wanted to sell it in the foreign exchange markets of the world. But since it was not convertible it fluctuated in value. Its fluctuations reflected changes in the balance of supply and demand on trade and capital accounts, or in men's expectations as regards the future.

The authorities, however, did not completely wash their hands of the development of the exchange rates of sterling, but intervened in the market through the 'Exchange Equalisation Account'. They came into the market in order to prevent short-term influences having overmuch effect on the quotations, to counteract speculation, and to offset movements of capital mainly actuated by political motives ('hot money'). This system appeared to work well; it covered the whole sterling area, and a number of other nations not formally linked to Britain attached themselves to the sterling system.

It has already been observed that both the United States and the United Kingdom were pursuing cheap money policies during this period with a view to reviving activity and employment. It was possible for the United States to combine this policy with a (partially) convertible dollar because of the large size of her gold reserves. She could be quite indifferent as to whether easy money might tend from time to time to create an adverse balance of payments; after 1933 the flow of capital to the United States further increased her reserve. It would have been quite impossible for Britain, for reasons that I have already explained, to combine that cheap money régime, which was so desirable from the domestic point of view, with a convertible sterling. Under the old British system that prevailed, so long as sterling was convertible, the external situation had to be the prime determinant of easy or tight money policy. The new system had much influence upon the thought that gave birth to the International Monetary Fund.

Meanwhile another system was growing up which restricted marketability itself. Under the pressure of the world slump, Germany had to declare a moratorium in 1931. Holders of German marks could no longer market them freely. Out of this situation there developed a complicated system of exchange control and multiple currency arrangements. Meanwhile for certain holders marks retained their old par value. At the official rate it soon came to be over-valued. By means of her control system, Germany was able to sustain the nominal value of the mark, despite heavy indebtedness, despite over-valuation, and in due course despite heavy expenditure on rearmament. The German system compelled her trading partners in many cases to take similar action, and a wide-reaching system of exchange controls, blocked currencies and clearings, imposed by one partner or agreed to by both, grew up. This involved violent kinds of discrimination and could be, and often was, made the weapon of political pressure. It was certainly restrictive in tendency, although trade has a wonderful way of surmounting formidable obstacles; it was also sinister in tendency.

I must now pass to the thinking which preceded the agreements designed to govern policy in a brave post-war world. The thinking began early owing to American initiative and was the direct consequence of the Lend-Lease arrangement. President Roosevelt said that when one's neighbour's house is on fire, one lends him a hose-pipe. Afterwards, presumably, he returns the hose-pipe. But the hose-pipe in this case was a multiplicity of miscellaneous objects from fighting aircraft and tanks to cotton and tobacco. How were all these to be returned? It was understood that it would be undesirable to encumber nations with heavy post-war indebtedness, a phenomenon which certainly gave trouble in the 'twenties and which some even believe to have been one cause of the great slump. It was understood accordingly that no dollar sign was ever to be put upon the supplies conveyed under Lend-Lease, so that there should be no question of repayment in money. (A dollar sign has indeed since been put upon them often enough; for statisticians the temptation was too great to be resisted.) How then were these things to be handed back? Tobacco that Britain does not grow, aircraft of obsolete design, or a smaller number of aircraft of equivalent value — but then the dollar sign would surely have to come in? The Americans had what seemed at first sight a brilliant idea. Let all question of a material return be waived, and instead let Britain be asked to accept certain principles of policy that were favoured by the United States. In exchange for material support during war there was to be a 'consideration' of a less tangible kind. It was certainly an ingenious idea, and at first glance seemed a welcome one to the harassed British sorely in need of still more supplies.

When one is asked to give a set of lectures named after a benefactor and in an honourable succession, one has some heightening of a sense of responsibility: one's thoughts take a graver turn. It may have been obvious for long to many British that this idea of a 'consideration' was not a good one. I did not appreciate this fully at the time, partly, it must be confessed, because broadly I approved of the policy which the British were asked to join with the Americans in implementing; but that was a shallow view. In what follows I will address myself particularly to any Americans who happen to con these words.

It is not a good idea to barter a subscription to a principle for a material consideration. For a material advantage one may surrender an island, a base, a fleet of ships; one may make tariff or trade concessions, always provided that they are specifically and clearly defined. To surrender a principle for money is not exchanging like with like, and is unsound.

The nature of this particular transaction may be interpreted in various ways. It might be held that the principles to be subscribed to were entirely in line with what the British intended to do anyhow. In this case the transaction has a bogus aspect. It could be argued that it was a way in which a far-sighted and humane American Administration could satisfy a less enlightened Congress. If this were the true interpretation, the real transaction was a purely internal American affair, and one impossible for an outsider to judge. But this is probably not the correct interpretation. It would be difficult to maintain that the Administration did not believe that the transaction would have some influence on what the British actually did.

If it did, there are still alternative interpretations. If

this agreement was to cause the British Government to pursue a continuing policy that would injure the interests and well-being of the British people, it was wrongful, for it would set up an intolerable conflict of duty. In the end the doctrine that *salus populi suprema lex* would be bound to prevail and the whole transaction would only have served to weaken the authority of international agreements.

A different interpretation is possible. It may be said that the 'consideration' did not require the government to do anything really injurious to its people, but merely constituted a kind of appeal to its better self. The principles set out, it could be argued, were entirely in accord with the long-term interests of the British people. The only trouble was that shorter views might prevail in a majority of democratically elected legislators. Thus the object of the transaction could be represented as being, not to make the government do anything contrary to the public interest, but rather to safeguard it from sectional pressures and party prejudices, to convince it that longer views should shape present policy. But that plea fails too, for it conflicts with Butler's immortal adage, which should be the overriding maxim in all international co-operation and international leadership :

> He that complies against his will
> Is of his own opinion still.

What was to be the line of policy? The opening thought here came from the Secretary of State, Mr. Cordell Hull, who had been putting up such a magnificent fight before the war to introduce a little liberalism into international commerce. Let the nations of the world dismantle their trade restrictions and discriminations.

I must dwell very briefly on this aspect, although it is not strictly germane to the currency question, and although it necessarily involves a controversial note, which I am loath to introduce into these lectures. It is necessary to do so because the issues involved have become tightly interwoven with problems concerning the dollar in its international aspect.

The substance of the consideration, as opposed to the bare idea of a consideration as such, was unconditionally welcome to the group, which had now become a minority in Britain, of what may be called out-and-out Free Traders. It can, I believe, also safely be said that it was broadly not unwelcome, subject to important reservations, to the majority. It was in line with the traditions of British policy. The protectionist party were only moderate protectionists. Britain depends so vitally on the fullest possible flow of world commerce that it is evident to most thinking people that any movement towards all-round liberalization must redound to Britain's advantage. There was an opposition, but it was decidedly a minority group, consisting of those in whose minds new ideas were taking shape for building up a self-supporting British bloc, by tightening the economic bonds of the Commonwealth and Empire and by gaining as many other adherents to its economic system as might be found.

All would agree that commitments entered into would have to be of deferred application, as severe and ruthless policies might be required during the awkward period of post-war reconstruction. Subject to this, the majority was favourable. But there were also other provisos.

Apart from the out-and-out Free Traders, who may well have been in unconditional sympathy with Mr. Hull, that majority which I have described as broadly in sympathy would have been inclined to comment as follows: 'That is a perfectly sound idea in itself; given the right environment such a policy should redound to the general advantage and to British advantage; but it makes no attempt to cope with the main problems that confront us; it is something of a fair-weather policy; but we have not had fair weather since 1929, or even since 1914; what is your policy to restore fair weather?' In this line of thought it was not simply the difficulties of the transitional period that weighed, but all those difficulties with which the world had been struggling before ever the war broke out. It may be that Mr. Hull thought that those difficulties were mainly due to restrictions on trade, and that, if these were removed, the weather would become fair again. With that view the majority of British were no longer in sympathy.

Before the International Economic Conference of 1933 Keynes wrote as follows in his *Means to Prosperity*:

For the Conference to occupy itself with pious resolutions concerning the abatement of tariffs, quotas, and exchange restrictions will be a waste of time. In so far as these things are not the expression of deliberate national or imperial policies, they have been adopted reluctantly as a means of self-protection, and are symptoms, not causes, of the tension on the foreign exchanges. It is dear to the heart of Conferences to pass pious resolutions deploring symptoms, whilst leaving the disease untouched.

This view may not have commanded majority assent in 1933; but it emphatically did so now. Hull's proposals were all very well, but they did not go to the root of the world's malaise; they were essentially secondary in character.

Another mental reservation may be discerned in the response of British public opinion to this initiative. Surely it was excessively paradoxical? What exactly was the United States doing in asking Britain to sub-scribe to the principle of greater Freedom of Trade, when the United States had been for the best part of a century a very highly protectionist country, while Britain during most of that period had adopted the uttermost Freedom of Trade, and even in the last few years had only been moderately protectionist. It did not appear to make sense. And thereby it became suspect.

And then there was another thought. Let us suppose that the American Administration was really sincere. Would it be in a position to implement this idea? From the point of view of a large new development towards greater freedom of trade in the world, it would be useless for the Americans to pare off some tariffs that were comparatively inessential and not effectively impeding trade very much. If the United States meant business, it would be essential for her to make tariff concessions of a kind that would admit British and other foreign goods in large quantity. This might be found to cause a considerable permanent loss to certain industries and some temporary distress to the whole economy. If the United States was to turn over a new leaf in tariff policy, it would be necessary for her to submit herself to a painful period of transition. The Administration may have already foreseen and faced all this; but was Congress in full agreement? Would Congress really pass legislation causing severe maladjustment in the American economy? Free trade may be good, but a country that has adopted high protection for many decades cannot suddenly go over to it without considerable self-sacrifice in the short period. The British people were frankly incredulous about this initiative. It just did not look right.

We have to go a little deeper. In the wording of the Mutual Aid Agreement, there is a reference to the 'reduction of tariffs' and to the 'elimination of all forms of discriminatory treatment'. There was a deliberate distinction here between 'reduction' and 'elimination'. This gave the proposal a special twist. One might think of the complex system of discrimination and its potentialities of political pressure that had been built up in Germany by Herr Schacht. Although there were a few who wished Britain to adopt a similar system as a

matter of permanent policy, and more who thought
that something of this sort might be inevitable during
the transition, there would not be difficulty in getting
British agreement in principle, if the Americans earn-
estly desired it, for the elimination of this kind of
discrimination.

It was understood, however, that discrimination also
covered Imperial Preference. This implied a criticism,
not of the enemy, but of an ally.[1] Anyhow, Imperial
Preference was a small-order affair compared with the
forbidding American tariff. An economist — and in
this matter an economist is not out of accord with common sense of the general public — judges tariffs, discriminations, etc., by the extent to which they prevent
beneficial trade from occurring. A tariff which pre-
vents much trade is more evil than a discrimination
that only affects a little trade.

That was common sense. But it was not the doctrine of the State Department. According to that doctrine, a tariff is merely an expression of nationalism,
which on the whole it has been prepared to bless in the
twentieth century; discrimination is an expression of
imperialism, which is an unmitigated evil. This was
age-old State Department doctrine.[2] Heavy stress, common sense would argue, on a movement towards greater
freedom of trade was good as far as it went, but failed
to attack the disease, and should be regarded as a sup-
plement to, rather than as constituting, the main line of
policy. But what of the emphasis on the distinction
between protection and discrimination? This was not
common sense; it was not economics; it was of minimum value either as a main line or a supplementary
policy; and it contributed nothing whatever to the

[1] It is fair to say that the main lines of this document were shaped
before Pearl Harbour.
[2] For a very clear and succinct statement of the principle, see *International Economic Policies*, by William S. Culbertson, 1925, pp. 185-6.

great problems of reconstruction which the world would soon have to face. In fine, it was not a contribution to the existing situation, but a mere piece of ideology, or, as some have preferred to call it, theology.

The principle was indeed a trivial matter in relation to the world scene; and its application to Imperial Preference was not acceptable to the British. While they might be prepared to agree in general to the desirability of non-discrimination, they would not apply it to Imperial Preference, as the unity of the Commonwealth and Empire alters the case. Furthermore, the ground of the principle was also unacceptable with its implication that imperialism in the sense intended is bad. British Imperialism, if it should be so called, has had in the recent period two aspects, being on the one hand an association of completely free nations under the Crown, and on the other the embodiment of the work, loyally carried out by the tireless and largely selfless efforts of many generations of British citizens, in providing at least some of the preconditions of civilization in primitive societies. The British regard this as something of unique value in world history, of which she is intensely proud. That remains valid to-day.

A few more words may be said about the State Department principle. It has roots deep in history, going back to the War of Independence. After victory, the United States found herself confronted with discriminations, such as the British Navigation Laws, in many parts of the world. She had to fight a long-continuing battle to secure just and equal treatment in all parts. The fight was a good one and has long since been crowned with the success that it deserves. If nations now adopt discriminations against imports from the United States, that is not out of any lack of respect or lack of desire to give fair and just treatment to American traders, but is simply due to lack of dollars. While we may admit that discrimination is wrong in principle and only justified by the necessities of the case, it is not something which at the present day is inflicting serious injury, if any injury at all, upon the United States economy. One may venture the opinion that the strength of her views in this matter is at least as much an anachronistic survival of the righteous war-cries of battles long ago, as it is a manifestation of theology.

One final word. The American principle of non-discrimination has been traditionally known in the history of economic diplomacy as 'unconditional most-favoured nation treatment' for all. This contrasts with 'conditional most-favoured nation treatment'. Under the former system if country B is accorded most-favoured nation treatment by A, any concessions made by A to other countries are automatically granted to B. Under the conditional form, a concession made by A to C in return for some other concession is not granted to B unless B makes to A a concession equivalent to that which C has made. If B is unwilling to do this, she will continue to receive less favoured treatment than C in A's market; in fact A justifies herself in continuing to discriminate against B. In her just and righteous campaign to secure proper treatment over many decades, the United States was only willing to allow 'conditional' most-favoured nation treatment; that means that she upheld the principle of discrimination in her own dealings. She may have felt, especially in the early days, that this was a weapon she could not relinquish. Throughout that time Britain and other European nations granted most-favoured nation treatment in its unconditional form. It was only after the First World War that the United States was won over to granting the unconditional form. In her own policy, non-discrimination has therefore been of very recent date. This is by no means a matter for blame. It is only to be noted that a recent convert sometimes holds theological doctrines with exceptional fervour.

While many would affirm that this type of thinking made no contribution to solving the problems that were about to confront the world, or at best but a microscopic one, it does not follow that it has had no value. The Americans have continued to press this point of view strongly. While causing irritation on account of its irrelevance, and of its apparent hostility to British ideals and achievements, it has none the less had a healthy influence. There is economic value in the unity of the British Commonwealth and Empire; this value does not and should not consist in diverting trade to any great degree from its natural channels. There is a school of thought, however, which, beglamoured by the imperial concept, has held that Britain should strive to create a self-sufficient bloc. This would certainly be contrary to the aims of the Atlantic Charter, contrary to long-run British interests, and probably· impracticable; but the mirage is always in danger of having a distracting influence. The resolute American opposition to discrimination has had· a steadying influence through a difficult period, and has helped to prevent Britain, somewhat unnerved by the great pressures to which she has been subject, from seeking escape down a wrong turning. To sum up, while I would maintain that the question of non-discrimination has made a nugatory contribution to the main problems, it has been justified to the extent that it has reduced the influence of enthusiasts for a wrong ideal.

If for a moment one were allowed to tolerate the notion of 'conditional' most-favoured nation treatment as advocated by the United States for many decades, and if one looks at the matter broadly, it would justify a good deal of discrimination against the United States. By the principle implicit in the conditional form, nations are entitled to have lower tariffs against other low-tariff nations than they have against high-tariff nations.

In view of all this, it is understandable that the

reaction to this part of the American initiative was not enthusiastic. Indeed if this had been the sole proposition put forward, it may be doubted if it would have found acceptance even in return for the material gain proposed. American thinking, however, is not confined to the high priests of the State Department. There were many Americans, not excluding Americans in the State Department itself, who were of the opinion that the question of discrimination was not the key to post-war reconstruction and the avoidance of world-wide depression. There were many who had thought deeply about the actual problems of the modern world. They were somewhat at a disadvantage. The Hull doctrine had the asset of having behind it tremendous departmental backing and experience drawn from past diplomacy. The others were groping after new ideas. It is hard enough for the cloistered academic to give forth a new idea appropriate to the occasion; how much worse for those involved in the daily routine of administration and distracted by the excitements of departmental power politics. While many men of distinction gave their minds to these problems, attention came to be focused on Harry White, not only because of his powerful intellectual grasp, but also because of his personal energy and firm resolve to bring his ideas on to the plane of international discussion and practical application. In him were united certain qualities required for successful emergence in the hurly-burly. Others may have had even better ideas; others may have had cooler judgement; others certainly had more acceptable methods of advancing and negotiating their views. Harry White conceived that some bold new departure was needed to revive the world's monetary system; he was fully convinced that the Hull recipe for post-war economic policy was not enough; and he did succeed in bringing his ideas into the forum of international discussion. Whether in his absence another would have come forward and achieved this result we cannot know; Harry White was successful and must have credit for that. What can be said is that, had it not been known in British circles that there was this initiative complementary to the Hull initiative, the British would have been reluctant to enter into the series of discussions that took place. As it was, they hoped that there was enough agreement of view to give value to forward-looking discussions at a time when the two nations were still brothers-in-arms. Thus Harry White played a part of no mean importance.

His role has since been denounced. This matter must be left for future historians. In an account of the dollar, it would be quite wrong not to accord him an honourable mention. It need not be denied that he had a starry-eyed view of the virtues of the Russian 'democracy'. Americans have some tendency to be starry-eyed about many things. This has its disadvantages, but on balance it is an amiable and fine quality which the world admires. White was thoroughly unorthodox in his methods; and his unorthodoxy may — for all I know — have extended to dealings with a then allied power. It is somewhat fatuous to stress the charge of communism against a man who devoted energies equal to those of five other men and wore out his constitution to the point of death in tireless efforts to strengthen the economy of his own country and those of the other freedom-loving countries. Many of those who knew him really well still regard it as unthinkable that he was in any sense disloyal to his country, or anything but a fine patriot. He was strongly anti-British and, from the point of view of the smooth progress of Anglo-American relations, he was a troublesome fellow. He was a trouble to some of his American colleagues also. It would be an exaggeration to call him a great American; but he was a distinguished and eminent and hard-fighting American.

In the early phase of consideration for the post-war problems, British thought was much influenced by its memory of the slump and the following years of depressed activity. The Hull solution was considered irrelevant. Mention may be made of Keynes, whose influence at this time was steadily growing. It is not implied that all his specific theories were accepted. Of that small circle who bent their minds to these problems, it may well be that some disagreed with Keynes' presuppositions, disagreed with his premises, disagreed with his modes of reasoning, disagreed with his conclusions and disagreed with his over-all theory, and yet held that by and large he was working in the right kind of direction. That such could be the state of affairs is merely a symptom of the vague and confused condition of economic science in relation to practical affairs. Meanwhile Keynes was the one person whose ideas were clearly defined and who could give them persuasive expression. Thus there was a tendency to adopt his thoughts provisionally as the best available.

His plan for a Clearing Union corresponds, albeit with much elaboration, to the scheme for an international gold note issue that he put forward in 1933.[1] This resemblance indicates that when he drafted the Clearing Union, his thought was still dominated by the problem of world-wide depression. His main recipe in the *Means to Prosperity* was a simultaneous and, as far as possible, a concerted expansion of investment in the various countries. To give nations the courage to go forward with ambitious plans and a wider margin of reserves to cover consequential disturbances in their balances of payments, he wished greatly to enlarge the quantity of internationally liquid assets. This was to be accomplished by the gold note issue. This corresponded to his proposal in his paper on the Clearing Union for an international currency to be called Bancor; but the Clearing Union plan was less expansionist.

British thinking was also influenced by the possibility

[1] Cf. *Means to Prosperity* already quoted.

that the United States would assume a continuing and, one might say, oppressive position as a creditor on current account in the international balance of payments.

An additional and separate problem, which bulked ever larger in the British mind as the war continued, was the fear that Britain would have an intractably adverse balance of payments. It is to be emphasized that this was something quite apart from the problems, then beginning to loom large, of what came to be thought of as the transition period. It was not merely that Britain, having allowed her exports to run right down, would have to make a tremendous build-up and would need aid to get back to a peace-time basis; there was a much deeper question. The evolution of a century had made Britain extraordinarily dependent upon foreign trade; by continuous enterprise that matched her growing needs she had managed to keep abreast in the precarious adventure of sustaining a dense population by the sale of their products abroad. It was expected that the war would produce a permanent alteration in the structure of international trade adverse to Britain, and that there would be a large leeway to make up. This would be something more than post-war reconstruction of a normal kind and involve compressing into a few years an amount of enterprise in securing an expansion of sales abroad that would normally only be encompassed in a generation. All these fears were amply confirmed by the actual course of events when the war was over. It was this prospect that made the more theological parts of the Hull initiative, namely those relating to Imperial Preference, appear especially untimely.

In the Clearing Union plan there was provision for the creation of a new medium of international liquidity, and there was provision for the preponderantly creditor nation problem. The former was partly explicit, namely

in the provision of Bancor, and partly only potential.
The fact that the Clearing Union — in this unlike the
International Monetary Fund — was to have the structure of a world central bank meant that it could be given
the power, should an occasion, such as a severe world
depression, demand it, to create credit without obtaining additional subscriptions from anyone. As regards
the credit nation problem, Keynes' idea was to dis-
tribute duties for curing an imbalance of payments more
fairly as between nations finding themselves on the
credit side and those on the debit side. The latter were
to be allowed some latitude in the form of quotas which
would embolden them in their internal investment plans
and make it less incumbent to impose import restrictions,
in the event of a world recession. In the last resort,
however, the plan was in line with the normal necessities of the human situation, in that the debit country,
having exhausted its quota, had to put its own house in
order. She was given some latitude by comparison
with the pre-war situation, but in the end had to face
her ineluctable task.

In the pre-war days there had been no sanction
against a country that allowed a persistently credit
position to remain. It could continue to suck in gold
from the rest of the world, possibly to the point of
creating a complete breakdown of the use of gold as a
medium of international settlement. The anxieties occa-
sioned by the drain of gold to the United States in
1921-4 had been revived by the experience of the late
'thirties. It is true that the size of the U.S. credit balance on current account had been much exaggerated in
many minds and that the extent to which the drain of
gold to the United States was due to a flight of capital
was not fully appreciated. Still there was a problem,
and it was expected to become more acute after the
war. This expectation also was justified. The sanction
against the credit country in the Clearing Union was

that, instead of receiving ever-growing quantities of gold, it would receive growing quantities of Bancor, which could be used for purposes of international payment only. The idea was that as the credit country became encumbered with an ever greater amount of Bancor, it would feel impelled to adapt its external policies in such a way as to reduce its credit position. Thus both debit and credit countries would have to play their appropriate parts in maintaining an even balance, while there would be considerable latitude on both sides.

This plan was greatly modified by being merged with Harry White's plan for a Stabilization Fund, which became the International Monetary Fund. The structure was radically altered, so that the latent possibility of creating credit to meet a world depression without drawing on new subscriptions was removed. The quotas were much reduced. The Americans refused to contemplate the solution that unless a persistently credit country took its own steps to rectify the situation, it would be burdened with an ever-growing amount of Bancor. They held that its liability must be strictly limited, and that it should in fact be limited to an amount equal to its quota (right of drawing upon the Fund).

The British had felt that the bold Keynes plan for creating liquidity would justify them in joining in the Hull initiative for the liberalization of commercial policy despite their prospective balance of trade difficulties. When the Keynes plan was transformed and re-emerged in a woefully shrunken form, there were grave doubts whether the new scheme was good enough. Still, we were living in a world full of dangers where great risks had to be taken, and it was felt, largely in consequence of Keynes' persuasion, that this risk was just acceptable.

There was one point on which the Americans made a very generous concession to help the British in their attitude in regard to persistently credit countries. This consisted in the 'Scarce Currency Clause', whereby the currency of a country maintaining a consistently credit position could be declared 'scarce' and other nations would then be allowed to discriminate against it. Thus if the rest of the world found itself in difficulties *vis-à-vis* the credit country, instead of being forced, as previously, to adopt either severe deflation leading to massive unemployment, or general import restrictions of a beggar-my-neighbour character likely to increase the difficulties of other debit countries, it could confine its restrictions to the imports emanating from the persistently credit country. The action of the International Monetary Fund in declaring a currency scarce would give a signal to all other countries, enabling them to maintain active and unrestricted trade with one another while discriminating against the scarce currency country only. This was certainly a helpful provision.

In the event of scarcity arising, it would be desirable to confine the extent of the discrimination to what was needed to secure an even balance, and not to allow licence to the rest of the world to discriminate without limit. It would also be important that the discriminations should be as universal as possible. In relation to the dollar, for instance, some countries are in normal, natural and permanent deficit, while others may be expected to be in surplus. If, owing to some general cause, there were an over-all shortage of dollars for the rest of the world, it would not be desirable for the whole onus of adjustment to be thrown on to the countries that are in normal deficit, while those in normal surplus were able to proceed as usual. The over-all scarcity of the dollar is a burden for the rest of the world, and each country should help carry the burden in proportion to its size and to the urgency of its need for the specific goods that it usually obtains from the United States. A little all-round discrimination against dollar goods should serve to bring the pattern of trade nearer the ideal equilibrium, than would intense discrimination by some countries combined with no discrimination by others.

In the Articles of Agreement of the International Monetary Fund there is an obnoxious clause which might be deemed to stand in the way of this correct procedure.

'They [limitations on the freedom of exchange operations in the scarce currency] shall be no more restrictive than is necessary to limit the demand for the scarce currency to the supply held by or accruing to the member in question.'[1]   These words violate the multilateral principle, which is supposed to lie at the base of the International Monetary Fund, and make the discriminations authorized in consequence of a currency becoming scarce a purely bilateral matter between each separate member and the scarce currency country.   Thus it would appear to preclude the proper operation of the scarce currency procedure, and to compel the countries in normal debit with the scarce currency country to do the lion's share, if not all, of the discrimination, while forbidding the countries that happen to be in normal credit with the scarce currency country to join in the general scheme.   This is an application of bilateralism of an objectionable kind.

No such words occur either in the scarce currency clause of White's original plan for a Stabilization Fund, or in the 'Joint Statement by Experts' issued after the main discussions between the Americans and British had been completed.

The austerities of the International Monetary Fund may be deemed to have been somewhat mitigated by the simultaneous creation of a Bank for International Reconstruction and Development.   This was designed to enlarge the flow of international investment and thereby

[1] Article VII, Section 3 (b).

enable countries to adopt those bolder plans which may be deemed necessary, not only for the advancement of less developed countries, but also to prevent world-wide depression. In the *Means to Prosperity* which can probably be regarded as a key to his more elaborate thoughts at a later phase, Keynes laid little stress on international investment — rather the contrary — holding that what was important was to encourage countries to be more active in their own investment pro-grammes. What was needed to give them the necessary encouragement to do so was not so much the provision of international lending as (1) the provision of a larger reserve of international liquidity, and (2) some assurance, through the intervention of an international agency, that each and all would go forward in step in their bolder investment plans, so that the tendency for each and every country to run into an adverse balance through its own larger spending would be offset by the simultaneous larger spending of the others. Keynes also held strongly that this general movement should be supported by the largest possible internal capital develop-ments in the mature countries, so that they would main-tain high activity at home, and consequently a high level of purchases from the less developed countries.

Much surprise has been expressed that Keynes did not show greater enthusiasm for the International Bank in the earlier phases of the discussions about it, since it seemed, on the face of it, to be so much in line with his advocacy of world-wide expansionism. I confess that I have myself been puzzled by this. I now suggest that the true answer is to be found in the *Means to Prosperity*. He saw difficulties and dangers in large international lending. The same result could be obtained by each and every country undertaking its own investment — by inflationary methods if you like — and by each and every country being protected against adverse reactions on its trade balance both by the existence of large

reserves whether of gold or Bancor, and by the knowledge that there was some international machinery for
getting the various countries to keep more or less in
step with one another in their pace of expansion.

Those concerned with the trade cycle and recurrent
depression have advocated that nations should have
plans for capital development, which would go forward
steadily through good and bad times, or might, to the
extent that it was possible, be arranged 'contracyclic-
ally' so as to provide supplementary demand in bad
times.   This idea would be appropriate also to the
investment policy of the International Bank.   It would
clearly be desirable that this Bank should be able to
give some assurance that there would not be a sudden
drying up of international lending such as occurred in
the year before the Wall Street crash of 1929.   I had
occasion to discuss these matters with White and suggested that I might usefully mention these points to my
British friends for inclusion in the draft scheme for the
Bank.   He begged me not to do so.   He entirely agreed
with the substance of my suggestions.   He put it that
'you and we' (the British and Americans) were in fact
going to run the Bank and would certainly see to it that
precisely these lines of policy were carried out in the
working of it.   But it would be inadvisable to have
such proposals embodied in the draft, as they might
frighten Congress.

One further point must be made in regard to the
International Monetary Fund.   The main structure of
the world currency system that it upholds consists of a
chain of currencies that have a fixed rate of exchange
with one another for the time being, it being allowable
to alter these rates from time to time to correct a
'fundamental disequilibrium'.   There is clearly here a
strong family resemblance to the British system in the
years 1932–9, when the authorities endeavoured to
obtain the greatest possible stability of the pound ster-

ling in foreign exchange markets in the face of seasonal fluctuations, temporary disequilibria and speculative movements, while allowing the exchange to move to a new level if this seemed necessary to secure long-term equilibrium. The greatest amount of short-period stability and such adjustments as are required by long-run equilibrium considerations: these seem to have been the objectives both of the British management of the Exchange Equalization Account before the war and of the founders of the International Monetary Fund. Unhappily, there is also a great difference. The British system was undefined and empirical and flexible; the International Monetary Fund system is rigid and clearly defined. The latter quality is probably necessary for a multi-national agreement. But this rigidity and this clear definition may be fatal defects. At any time it probably passes the wit of man to know whether a given rate of exchange is appropriate to the long-run equilibrium or not; the British system allowed progress by trial and error. It also gave the authorities fairly complete power to outmanœuvre the speculators; if sterling was under pressure, they could allow it to drop to a level at which the speculators could not be sure whether the further movement was likely to be upwards or downwards. Under the International Monetary Fund system, the changes are formal and notified, and there is some desire to avoid having too many. A decision may be deferred too long; during this period there may be speculation all going one way; when the time for the final decision comes, too great a change may be made to prevent the necessity of further changes and to kill speculation. Above all, the decision has to be final — final anyhow as regards the year or two ahead — ; under the British system there never had to be a final decision ; a tentative reduction could always be followed by a correction ; and, as there are never adequate grounds for a final decision, it is unsatisfactory that there should have to be one. Under the Articles of Agreement of the Fund nations have limited rights of making unilateral changes within 10 per cent.; but it was hoped that the normal procedure would be to make a change only after consultation with the Fund, and that the limited right of unilateral decision would be confined to occasions of an exceptionally severe and sudden crisis or to those — which it was hoped would be still more exceptional — when the member country was at hopeless loggerheads with the Fund. In Keynes' original draft for a Clearing Union he proposed a much better plan. It is clear that he had the idea that the decision to execute change would normally lie with the nation itself; good order was to be maintained by the provision that no nation should make a change of more than 5 per cent. in any one year. Five per cent. per annum should be quite enough to correct fundamental disequilibrium in normal circumstances. The 5 per cent. per annum right would be cumulative, and, over a term of years, give a far wider margin than the right of a once-over unilateral adjustment of 10 per cent. allows. Such a plan would retain all the flexibility and other advantages of the pre-war British system; there could be tentative movements up or down within the limits; there would be means of outwitting speculators; there need be no finality. Five per cent. would be amply sufficient, save on occasions of some great economic upheaval. In that case a larger change might be desirable, and it is then that consultation with the International Monetary Fund would be required. That would have been a workable plan for combining flexibility and stability.

The merits of the plan that was actually accepted and embodied in the Articles of Agreement of the International Monetary Fund cannot yet be known. The aftermath of war has entailed greater maladjustments than were anticipated, and there has been a prolonged 'transitional' period in which it has not been possible for the International Monetary Fund to operate in the normal way. It has been perforce somewhat quiescent. Will it later come to life?

Two conditions seem essential, if it is to fulfil the function of being an important aid to the liberalization of international trade, as originally envisaged. (1) It must be made absolutely clear that once the transition period is over, the drawing rights will be automatic. If they are not automatic, they do not constitute an addition to international liquidity at all. (2) It must be made absolutely clear that if ever a currency becomes scarce, as the dollar is now, it will be declared scarce without any hesitation. No doubt there are many other matters in which changes in its constitution have been rendered desirable in the light of experience, including an enlargement of its resources. But the two points mentioned are basic, and are pre-conditions for everything else. If these are not realized, then the main objectives of the war-time discussions will altogether fail of realization, and other methods will have to be sought in due course.

The establishment of the International Monetary Fund is an episode in the history of the dollar. United States membership entails rights and duties and affects the very nature of the dollar; for instance, the dollar is now a currency which may at any time, subject to the voting of members of the Board, be declared scarce.

It is not yet clear whether one setting out in the year A.D. 2000 to give a history of the dollar in four lectures will deem that the International Monetary Fund ought to be mentioned. Some matters have to be omitted for lack of space. If the institution develops in accordance with the ideas of its founders, then it is bound to get a very large mention in that short history.

Some anxiety must remain. Sustained and prodigious efforts seem necessary to secure notable advances in the monetary sphere. One only has to think of the inception of the Federal Reserve System. Hamilton's efforts were rendered vain after his death. Too many years passed before anything further was effected, but later there was a return to the charge, and after great endeavours and great frustrations, the Federal Reserve System was in the end achieved; that has proved a great achievement; it has endured, and is likely to continue to do so. We may be sure that in the end the United States, along with other co-operating nations, will achieve some form of central banking organization of world ambit, just as it was always certain that in the end Hamilton's vision would be realized. But it is impossible here and now to see what troubles are in store and what difficulties will have to be overcome before we attain a durable central banking system for the world.

IV

THE DOLLAR GAP

SINCE the war there has been much despondency. Currencies have remained inconvertible and in consequence, while the International Monetary Fund has carried out some useful operations, the system, of which it was intended to be the guardian, has not come into effect. The Bank for International Reconstruction and Development has proceeded further with the duties proposed for it. But it cannot be said that the plans of Bretton Woods have yet reached fulfilment. Nor has the other branch of the policy been more successful; Mr. Hull had hoped that there would be a clearance of restrictions and discriminations by comparison with the state of affairs prevailing at the outbreak of war; in fact the movement has been in the opposite direction. It was always understood that the transition period would give rise to special problems. It was not intended that the new institutions should be unduly burdened with these problems, thereby perhaps getting waterlogged before their normal operations had started. Transitional difficulties were to be catered for first by U.N.R.R.A., and then, when it seemed that its operations would not be adequate, by special loans, most notably the loan to Britain. When by 1947 the reconstruction of Europe was still far from complete, the great concept of Marshall Aid was formulated. For a period indeed the difficulties of the transition seemed to grow rather than to decline, and the time needed for dealing with them was prolonged again and again.

It may be well to consider at this point whether these so-called transitional problems were adequately formulated. A distinction ought to be made between two rather different types of problem. The transition in its purest sense might be regarded as the interval which the war-shattered economies needed for re-establishing production at, or moderately above, their pre-war levels, and re-establishing sales in export markets. Forces had to be demobilized, certain essential repairs to war-damaged capital carried out and industrial plant reorganized and re-equipped for peace-time production instead of arms output. In fine it was necessary for the economies to get back to somewhere near where they had been before the war broke out. While all this was going on, their citizens would have had to endure severe privations had not the United States, which had a greater margin of productive potential, come forward and offered aid of unprecedented generosity. Thus the turn-over to peace-time production was effected with less sacrifice and misery than would otherwise have been inevitable.

There was another distinct set of problems. When men and women were back at work, when the supply of materials had begun to flow normally, when the shipping potential was restored, when factories were in their normal working order, and when contacts in export trade had been re-established, would the position then be set fair? Would the transition then be over? Events have shown that the answer to these questions must be in the negative. The war caused great shifts in the pattern of world trade. A return to the pre-war productive potential and to pre-war exportation was not to mean a restoration of equilibrium. The relative position of Europe had deteriorated. For her it was not simply a question of re-establishing production and exportation, but of facing a new set of permanent problems; she would have to make great structural changes by comparison with the pre-war situation, and particularly to win large new markets abroad. Should this further set of problems be classified as transitional problems? To the extent that they were part of the aftermath of war they could be so regarded. But they were truly of quite a different character from the other set of problems. The former consisted of demobilization in the widest sense of the term. The latter imposed the need for new kinds of enterprise. The former could quite certainly be solved, given time; but the latter involved an element of uncertainty and would only be satisfactorily solved, if fortune favoured.

We may give this question of classification point by relating it to the new international institutions. They were designed to help the economies of the free world to function more smoothly and with less restrictions on trade. They were not primarily intended to give aid to countries suffering temporary impoverishment during the period of demobilization. But were the institutions of Bretton Woods and G.A.T.T. designed to assist in the great structural transformation that was also required? I do not believe that they were. Are they fitted to cope with that set of problems? It seems doubtful. Those institutions are designed to deal with the régime that will exist after post-war equilibrium has been fully established, to prevent ruptures in that equilibrium, to tide over the normal transitions of peace-time and to prevent the occurrence of serious depressions. This was surely how their authors conceived them and how they are adapted to function. Separate machinery was required, so those authors thought, for the transition. But their idea of the transition appears to have been inadequate. For them, the transition was the phase of demobilization in the widest sense. But what about the permanent structural readjustments? Problems connected with these do not appear to have entered into their thinking. This may have been responsible for certain confusions of thought that have subsequently prevailed, irritation on the part of some who hoped for a quicker achievement of a liberal multilateral system, and a sense of frustration and despondency on the part of others who begin to doubt if such an ideal can ever be realized.

It is not our purpose to range over all the structural problems; we are concerned specifically with the dollar aspect. The 'dollar gap', as it is called, is clearly a prominent feature.

In the period 1946–8 it was reasonable to represent the dollar gap as mainly due to overspending and inflationary pressures in the non-dollar countries. In particular, many countries were spending more on capital account than their citizens were saving. In part this was a natural characteristic of the demobilization process. Some held that certain countries were at fault in not curbing capital expenditure more strictly, and I myself took that view very strongly. It seemed to me absurd to complain of the dollar shortage when many of the countries were themselves creating it by overspending on capital account. This overspending appeared likely to generate an insolvency crisis of a most acute kind in 1947, and would undoubtedly have done so but for the great project of Marshall Aid.

This question of overspending on capital account was not altogether free from controversy. There were those who argued that it was so important from a longer view to have extensive capital reconstruction, that it was worth running the risk of short-term bankruptcy. To my judgement this was inverting the correct order of procedure. It seemed to me that the first thing to do was to establish solvency by putting every effort into exports. In most — not all — of the countries there was already enough capital for everyone to be fully employed; the capital might not be of the best; but it was working and would do. Let the product of the labour and capital available go as a first priority into export markets, and, as this could not be combined with the capital build-up that some desired, let capital reconstruction be postponed. If capital expenditure were drastically cut to the barest minimum, inflationary pressure could be reduced and even eliminated, and export markets could be cultivated and deliveries to them made prompt. Thus could the countries of Europe establish surpluses on external account as a first condition to further progress. But in Britain it was thought needful to spend money on the reconstruction of basic industries. In France M. Monnet produced an interesting plan which received much praise at the time. From my own point of view it appeared a fatal error. It must be confessed that American opinion was somewhat ambivalent. It was certainly critical of inflationary policies, while seeming to give strong support for large plans for capital reconstruction; yet really the former were identical with the latter. However, Marshall Aid made it possible for countries, for the time being and to a limited extent, to have the best of both worlds, to carry on with more capital outlay than they could have afforded from their own resources without incurring an immediate crisis of external insolvency.

The diagnosis for the dollar gap as it existed in the period from 1946 to 1948 was that it was a symptom of overspending on capital account, or, in other words, a symptom of inflationary pressure. In due course the inflationary pressure was reduced and in some countries eliminated, and the dollar gap was greatly reduced. I would suggest that, subject to exceptions, the inflationary period came to an end in 1951. In 1947 the dollar deficit of the world with the United States on current account was approximately $11 billion; in the three-year period 1950–52 it was approximately $2 billion p.a.[1] (My calculations give the figure of $2188 million.)

[1] I omit from the deficit the value of military items sent under defence programmes. Apart from these, I reckon in all forms of aid as being part of the deficit. The deficit is the actual excess of the value of goods and services received over those rendered. Defence aid (following E.R.P.) was one method by which this deficit was financed.

Let it be granted that the dollar deficit as it manifested itself in the early years was primarily caused by inflations elsewhere. It must not be inferred that the elimination of inflations elsewhere would automatically eliminate the deficit. A country may have no internal inflation and yet not achieve an external balance. This propostion must be regarded as fundamental.[1] (It is not inconsistent with the proposition that sufficient deflation can cure any deficit, provided that one is willing to tolerate an unlimited amount of unemployment.)

By the 'fifties the dollar gap had been reduced in a satisfactory way, but some gap remained. It must further be noted that the gap might have been considerably larger in 1950–52 had countries not maintained discriminatory restrictions on dollar purchases. These were inconsistent with the liberal system that it was hoped to establish. There was every prospect that, if United States aid was altogether terminated, the restrictions would have to be increased. This would involve moving in the opposite direction from that envisaged in the Hull initiative. How was this to be avoided? Open insolvency is clearly not an acceptable solution. While some inflationary tendencies were still present in certain countries, it no longer appeared plausible to suppose that the elimination of what remained would have a powerful enough effect by itself to cure the dollar shortage, which was mainly concentrated on Europe. There was no question of pressing on with deflation to the point of creating massive unemployment. It must be clearly understood that if the choice were between massive unemployment and the imposition of discriminatory restrictions, the latter would be preferred.

There are some who think that if the non-dollar world is determined to avoid massive unemployment, as it is, we shall have discriminatory restrictions on dollar imports as a permanent feature. That is not my opin-

[1] R. F. Harrod, *International Economics*, 2nd ed., pp. 132-4.

ion. But I would not urge that we can pass easily and quickly to a non-discriminatory régime. Adam Smith, who remains the greatest Free Trader, held that the dismantling of protective restrictions must be a slow process.

When we look back over the longish periods in which countries maintained their external balances without modern restrictive devices, we must remember that during these periods changes in basic conditions were proceeding by gradual stages. The free open system may have been adequate to adapt the balances to changes so proceeding. It does not follow that this same system has the power to secure quick adjustment to a vast change of conditions that is concentrated in a few years. Within the era of modern banking we just have not the experience of how an open trading system can adjust itself to such changes as those caused by the Second World War. We have the experience of the economically smaller event of the First World War, and that gave rise to much trouble and embarrassment.

There is an important exception to the general proposition that great economic changes have proceeded gradually over a course of years by fairly small steps. Sudden large maladjustments have been due to the incidence of booms and slumps. It has been recognized that these have imposed severe strains on the normal process of adjustment, and it is precisely for this reason that much thought has been given to this problem, and that it was felt necessary in the discussions during the Second World War to provide special mechanisms to cope with it. But that still leaves the other kind of problem uncatered for, namely how a free open trading system can adapt itself to the kind of large sudden change of circumstances that may be caused by such an event as the Second World War.

We have said that the first recipe offered by advocates of open trading for the post-war imbalance was to remove inflationary pressure. That removal has proved a very powerful recipe and produced a large cure; but the cure has not been complete. Advocates of open trading have a second recipe in their stock — the devaluation of the currencies of countries in deficit. This doctrine may be found expounded with much elaboration in the great treatise by Professor J. E. Meade [1] and by other modern writers. These writers do not present devaluation as a certain panacea, but only as a probable remedy. It is curative only on the assumption that there is sufficient elasticity in the demand and supply of commodities entering into the nation's external trade. Professor Meade holds that as a general rule we may expect sufficient elasticity. I do not challenge this. I believe it to be correct that in relation to the normal developments of peace-time, there should be enough elasticity for alterations in exchange rates to remedy maladjustments. Consequently, I would hold that the system envisaged at Bretton Woods whereby an imbalance on the deficit side is to be cured not by deflation, nor by trade restrictions, discriminatory or other, but by a moderate revaluation of the currency, is sound and adequate for the ordinary purposes of peace-time.[2]

It is not inconsistent with this to doubt whether elasticities can be expected to be sufficient where there is a large imbalance due to large changes in world conditions concentrated within a few years. About this we must preserve an open mind. It is to be remembered that a considerable part of modern trade is in processed articles, which are marketed, not in impersonal organized markets, but through trading channels created

---

[1] *The Theory of International Economic Policy*, vol. i : *Balance of Payments.*

[2] I hold that such a revaluation should be rotated to 'a fundamental disequilibrium' (to use the words of the Articles of Agreement of the I.M.F.) that is diagnosed as likely to endure through good and bad years alike. Deficits due solely to cyclical depression should be met by drafts upon the Fund — although it must be admitted that the Fund, as now constituted, is not likely to be large enough for that purpose.

over a term of years by zealous salesmanship and the establishment of the relations of goodwill. In such cases buyers are not always ready to substitute one source of supply for another at short notice in response to moderate price differentials.

Unhappily, the whole prospect of experimenting carefully with devaluation as a possible remedy for what remains of the dollar gap has been ruined by the excessive and ill-timed devaluation of sterling and a number of other currencies in 1949. In my judgement this was one of the greatest follies in the whole troubled course of monetary history. It is sometimes argued that this devaluation was not a matter of choice, but was forced upon the currencies concerned. This may have been so if one looks only at the few weeks that preceded it, when sterling was under severe speculative pressure. This adverse speculation was in large part due to the loose talk that had been proceeding all through the earlier part of 1949. If it had been formally stated by the International Monetary Fund and by the U.S. Treasury that devaluation was an utterly inappropriate remedy in the circumstances, and if the British had not only indicated, as they did, that they were averse to devaluation, but also that they were taking alternative positive measures to rectify the situation, the speculation would never have gathered momentum. Furthermore, in the last resort, the British could have avoided devaluation, despite all the adverse speculation, by restricting drawings upon non-resident sterling balances. Such action was envisaged in the Loan Agreement of December 1945. It might have been unfortunate to take such action in 1949, yet better than to agree to devaluation.

To begin with, this devaluation occurred at a time when inflation was still proceeding in most of the countries concerned. The correct policy was first to eliminate the inflation and then, that done, to see what kind of deficit remained. No one knows what the deficits would have been had the various countries been able to cultivate their export markets assiduously and to deliver promptly; internal inflationary pressures were making this impossible. Devaluation, by enlarging demand on export account, intensified inflationary pressure at home. It was a trifle absurd to stimulate new export demands by offering goods at lower prices when one could not even deliver the goods that were demanded at the old prices. The proceeding not only increased the strain upon industry, but also caused a spiralling of prices which I shall describe presently.

It should be laid down as a rule for those contemplating the use of this recipe, that it should only be used by a country which has already eliminated internal inflation. Now it may be said that this rule cannot be without exception. For inflation may have already gone so far that the whole structure of costs and prices inside a country has become manifestly out of line with world costs and prices, and that some devaluation is rather urgently required merely to record a *fait accompli* and to prevent its export prices becoming prohibitive. In a general way, this must be allowed. But the argument was not applicable to the British case in 1949. For this purpose we may compare the price and cost structure of the United Kingdom with that of the United States in 1948 against the year 1938. To allow for the sterling devaluation of 1939, I have multiplied U.S. 1948 price indexes by 1·2. In 1948 the U.S. general price index stood at 252 while the U.K. general price index stood at 216; in 1948 the U.S. wage index stood at 261 while the U.K. wage index stood at 179; the U.S. export price index stood at 250 while the U.K. export price index stood at 244. Thus all along the line prices expressed in sterling at 4·03 dollars had risen substantially more in the United States than in the United Kingdom in 1948. Thus it cannot possibly be said that the internal price and cost structure in the United Kingdom had got so out of line with that in the United States as to render a large devaluation necessary to record a *fait accompli*. It is true that U.S. export prices were pared down during the early part of 1949, probably in consequence of the recession there, which proved temporary. But one does not make a vast currency change on the basis of an experience lasting a few months only. The devaluation was not the record of a *fait accompli*, but an experiment with a method alleged likely to improve the external dollar balances of the devaluing countries.[1] Such an experiment should never be conducted in a country suffering from inflationary pressure.

Secondly, the Meade requirement for sufficient elasticity of supply and demand was much less likely to be realized in 1949 than in normal times, since it depends on elasticities both on the side of exports and of imports. In Britain imports were rigidly controlled, and there was thus likely to be little elasticity on that side, so that the whole curative effect, if any, of the devaluation, depended on the elasticity of demand for exports.

Thirdly, the devaluation was much too large. If a devaluation of this size was to be successful, it presupposed a vast expansion of exports, which was not only inherently improbable on the side of markets, but was rendered more so by the fact that the internal economy was already so strained that it could not possibly execute such an increase. There was a reason, however, which within its limits was good, for the large size of the devaluation. Sterling had been suffering from bear speculation. It was desired to make quite sure that this was brought to an end and it seemed to many that the only way of doing so was to have such a large devaluation as to convince everyone that there was no likelihood of there being another. From the point of view of speculation, the result achieved may have been

[1] The external trade of the United Kingdom was already at this time in *even* over-all balance.

satisfactory. Its effect on the general economic situation, including the balance of trade, was another matter. The dilemma with which the adverse speculation presented our authorities raises the whole question of the International Monetary Fund system. The need for the large-scale change was solely due to the rigidity of that system. If the British authorities thought that it would be advantageous to experiment with some reduction in the exchange value of sterling — waiving for the moment the danger of doing so during an inflationary period — it would have been desirable for them to proceed tentatively by small changes and by trial and error. The speculators would have been kept wondering. The authorities might indeed have found that a rate of 3·8, or even 3·5, was more satisfactory than one of 4·03 ; or they might not have found that. The thing could have been tested out fairly. If we regard the International Monetary Fund mechanism as a formalization of the principles of the Exchange Equalization Account, we have to ask whether in the process of formalization the virtues of the latter system have not been lost. This must be on the agenda for consideration by world opinion and by world monetary authorities, who in due course will have to re-examine the whole mechanism from a long-run point of view.

Devaluation caused a strong upward movement of the sterling prices of British imports. Analysis has been rendered difficult by the outbreak of the Korean war a year later ; there has been a tendency, which has sometimes seemed almost perverse, not to look back beyond that event to the effects of devaluation which were larger and more lasting. Already by June 1950 the prices that the British had to pay for imports had risen by 18 per cent. against 1948 ;[1] they would have risen more had the British position not been protected by long-term contracts. What one might logically expect would

[1] International Financial Statistics : International Monetary Fund.

be for those prices eventually to rise by 44 per cent. save to the extent that world prices expressed in dollars fell. But they did not fall at that time, nor have they even yet fallen below their level prior to devaluation.

Granted this rise in import prices, it was both inevitable and desirable that there should be an upward adjustment of internal prices in Britain. The British dependence on imports is so great that her general price level moves very closely with import prices. It could be argued that, since the object of devaluation was to improve the British competitive position, it was essential to prevent wages rising at all. This notion does not make sense in relation to so large a devaluation; to hold wages (and salaries, etc.) fixed in the face of a rise of import prices of 18 per cent. would involve a lowering of the standard of living of some 3 or 4 per cent. If wages were to be kept fixed in the face of the still greater rise of import prices that was bound to be caused eventually by devaluation, that would have entailed a still further fall in the standard of living. Any such lowering would have been quite out of relation to what was required by the situation; British labour would not have stood for it, and would have been fully justified in resisting it. It is to be remembered that in the year prior to devaluation, the British over-all external balance was already in equilibrium; a favourable balance was required, say, of £200 or £300 million. The dollar balance was showing a running deficit (offset by surpluses elsewhere) of some £300 million. Phenomena such as these do not call for a large over-all reduction in the standard of living; reductions of more than 5 per cent. belong to the realm of events that only occur in response to a major war or calamity of catastrophic dimensions.

And so an upward spiral of internal prices and wages was set going in Britain. This was most unfortunate. The British had during their transitional period relied much on voluntary restraints in regard to wages, profit distributions, price fixing, etc. Discipline was well maintained. In the two-year period prior to mid-1950 — the point of time at which the rise in the cost of living due to the surge of import prices began to be seriously felt — the average of British wages had only risen by 4 per cent., certainly by less than the increase of labour productivity. There are certain objections to a policy which relies on 'restraint' by individuals; the balance of argument, however, is in its favour in times of war or large post-war reconstruction. By mid-1949 Britain was nearing the end of the transition period, and there is reason to suppose that, but for the large devaluation, it would have been possible to hold the line until the termination of the special pressures of transition, after which prices could have been allowed to find their own way to a natural level. The British system of restraint was wantonly ruptured, and spiralling forces were set in motion, which have continued to this day (1953). Once a system of discipline and restraint, on which confidence is based, is broken, it is very difficult to re-establish it. We cannot yet measure the loss. This story has been developed in relation to Britain, but it is largely applicable also to the other countries of Europe that were involved in the devaluation.

This progress of events has also led to a bad diagnosis in recent times. An upward movement of internal prices may be due to internal inflationary pressures and was so in the post-war quinquennium. The upward movement of prices constituting an adjustment to a rise of import prices is of an altogether different character. The presence of the latter has tended to cause a false inference, especially in the last two years, that there were internal forces of inflation at work. The upward movement of import prices caused by devaluation was reinforced by the world-wide price movement following the Korean outbreak. By June 1951, the top of the post-Korean boom, British import prices had risen 58 per cent. against 1948. It is very difficult to say how far the rise during this year (mid-1950–mid-1951) was due to a further adjustment to devaluation, and how far to the Korean war. The rise in U.S. import prices of 36 per cent. may suggest that the relative British rise of 18 per cent. that occurred before Korea was not increased. This interpretation is not certain, however, since U.S. imports consist of a narrower range of more price sensitive goods. The movement of the general price index may be more significant. By June 1951 the U.K. general price index was 46 per cent. above the level of 1948; this was the natural reflection of the rise of 58 per cent. in her import price level. But U.S. general prices were only 10 per cent. above the 1948 level, although her import prices were 36 per cent. up. This is consistent with the far smaller dependence of the United States on imports. If we compare the U.K. general price index of 146 with the U.S. general price index of 110, we may judge that the difference gives a rough representation of the effect of devaluation upon the British price structure. The inevitability of internal upward retail price and wage movements in the United Kingdom is obvious. It is interesting to observe, however, that British sterling wages have risen less since 1948 than U.S. dollar wages. It seems probable that sterling is still somewhat under-valued (1953).

To those who argued that all these evils had to be endured in order to secure the desired effect of a stimulation of British exports to the United States, the result must have been extremely disappointing. It is in the field of manufactured goods that one looks for the effect of price elasticity upon the value of business done. U.S. imports of materials depend rather on her requirements, which in turn depend on the level of activity of her industry. Between 1948 and 1950, the value of British exports of finished manufactures to the United States rose from $165 million to $173 million.[1] This rise was considerably less than that of the U.S. national income during the period. It was compounded of an increase in the volume of British exports to the United States of about 31 per cent. and a reduction in the dollar prices at which they were sold (made possible by devaluation) of about 20 per cent. Thus devaluation appears to have had a nil or negligible effect on the value of British exports to the United States. In the following years their value has increased substantially. But before this happened, their dollar prices had already been marked up again, partly in consequence of the upward movement of internal costs of raw materials, labour, etc. Already in 1951 the prices that the British were asking the United States for their exports had risen by 17 per cent. on 1950.

If the gain of dollar income flowing from devaluation was meagre, it was not achieved without considerable effort. The overstrained British economy had in 1950 to send 31 per cent. more goods to the United States for the sake of a negligible return. If this had been the end of the story, it would not have mattered much, since she does not export a great quantity to the United States in any case. But this stimulus to send more exports without getting a compensating return applied to the whole vast range of her exports round the world, and was a burden upon her over-extended manufacturing capacity that was larger than the rearmament programme itself. It may have been supposed by some that the main effect of devaluation would be to alter the relation between the dollar prices of European exports and the dollar prices of U.S. exports, thus allowing a favourable change in the dollar balance. The main effect was somewhat different. It was to raise the prices, expressed in European currencies, of commodities

[1] *The Pattern of United States Import Trade Since 1923*, Federal Reserve Bank of New York (1952).

of world price quotation, which on the whole Europe has to import, against the prices of finished manufactures which Europe exports. The 'terms of trade' which had already moved substantially against Europe by 1948 compared with before the war, moved against her again, and this was a great burden. It is true that this second adverse movement was in part the effect of the Korean outbreak, and it may well be that the effects of the devaluation and those of the Korean outbreak will never be disentangled. It seems clear that the devaluation imposed a substantial additional burden.

It has been necessary to make what appears to have been a digression from the story of the dollar because the incorrect devaluation of 1949 has a profound effect on prospects. A dollar imbalance remains. The curative effect of disinflation may be held to be largely exhausted, on the assumption that the powers will not be willing to carry deflation to the point of causing massive unemployment. The second weapon envisaged in the war-time discussions about a world of liberal multilateral trading, devaluation, has been completely spoilt for the time being by a wrong use of it. It is idle to refuse to scrutinize this second point. People are apt to say, 'well, the devaluation may have been wrong; but it is over and done with now; it is probably too late to reverse it; so let us forget about it'. That may be good enough as an empirical attitude. But the Americans are deeply interested in the re-establishment of what is sometimes called a 'one world' system, and are restive at the prolongation of discriminations against dollar exports. Their attitude in this regard compels us to look at first principles, and in the realm of first principles the question of devaluation or, as it is sometimes called, 'the establishment of realistic exchange rates', is central. That is the essential remedy upon which in this ideology we rely, after the curative effects of disinflation have been exhausted. The spoiling of this weapon, therefore, cannot be regarded as irrelevant, as something past and done with, to be hushed up and forgotten about. A major step was taken, cutting us off from the use of this remedy for a number of years ahead.

This weapon having been dashed from our hands, it seems that nothing is left but the age-old one of restriction. Furthermore, it is clear that by restriction in this context we must mean discriminatory restriction. It would be absurd for Britain, which is in over-all external balance and, if we average good years with bad, has been in over-all external balance since 1947, to be compelled to impose all-round restrictions that were so severe that she came into dollar balance without having to discriminate against dollar imports. If she had to impose all-round restrictions of such severity as that, she just could not carry on. This argument applies to most of the other European countries.

There seems nothing for it then but to continue with the discriminatory system, and to wait for the gradual processes of adaptation, working slowly, to bring about a state of affairs in which discrimination will no longer be necessary. This is not to rule out completely the possibility of bringing back into use the devaluation remedy at some future date. If this was ever to be done, there would probably be a desire to use the method employed by the Exchange Equalization Account of tentative, provisional, reversible, small, stage-by-stage reductions, subject to trial and error and the power of the authorities to influence the movement by applying their resources in the market from time to time, rather than by the International Monetary Fund system of a once-over movement in the parity. Even this provisional method would not be acceptable to Britain so long as she is in the peculiar situation consisting of a combination of (a) a pressure on her dollar account and (b) an under-valuation of sterling.

It is next proper to ask what the causes are of this maladjustment in the balance that is giving so much trouble. For a period after the war the most important answer could be expressed in the words 'inflationary overspending'. That period is now over.

There are a number of reasons why the outside world has built up a larger demand for U.S. exports. Many are very familiar and I need not go over them. Troubles in the Far East, the Iron Curtain, and industrializing tendencies in certain countries that might otherwise have strongly expanded food production, have made the world more dependent on American food supplies. Large investment programmes have created demands for capital equipment that the United States has been well qualified to supply. More generally, the ability of the U.S. economy to meet foreign needs in the post-war quinquennium, when potential competitors in Europe were overstrained by the multitude of their additional tasks, may have enabled American producers and traders to build up customer connections, which, once formed, are not easily altered. There has also been a large shift in 'invisibles' in favour of the U.S.

There is one special cause of imbalance that I propose to dwell upon, because it is the biggest cause, and because it has been insufficiently stressed by others.

We have seen that ever since the 1870's the United States has had a rather large surplus on visible foreign trade account. At first this was used to buy back investments made by European capitalists in the United States; in the 'twenties it was used by the Americans to make investments in Europe; until the Second World War part of it was offset by a net U.S. deficit on invisible account; ever since the big gold-mining developments in South Africa, it has been partly used to purchase a share of newly mined gold. If we examine the 'thirties, when international investment was in the doldrums, we find an interesting pattern. In the six-year period 1933-8, the average annual gold production out-side the United States and the U.S.S.R. was $804 million.[1] Experts have computed that about 5 per cent. of this had to be earmarked for industrial uses.[2] This leaves $764 million of newly mined gold for monetary use. The amount required to balance the U.S. surplus on goods and services account, supposing that there had been no capital movement at all, was $267 million annually. Thus the rest of the world could finance its deficit by sending a suitable proportion of the newly mined gold to supplement American reserves, while retaining a larger share to supplement its own. The amount of gold actually sent to the United States per annum was $1140 million. This was owing to the large capital movement, whether attracted by prospects in the U.S. economy, or fleeing from the insecurities of Europe. Thus the gold reserves of the rest of the world were depleted and the United States had what appeared to be an unwelcome accession. This was not a well-balanced arrangement. It is to be observed that the deficit of the rest of the world with the United States was concentrated upon Europe, which was able, without great difficulty, to earn newly mined gold by having regular surpluses in other quarters, notably in the outer sterling area.

Had gold production outside the United States and the U.S.S.R. continued to increase, as it did steadily until 1940, or, to take a more pessimistic hypothesis, had it merely been sustained at the 1940 level ($1094 million), and had the dollar price of gold risen roughly in line with the world dollar prices of commodities generally, we should expect the newly mined gold avail-able each year for monetary use to be running around

[1] All the following gold figures are taken from the Reports of the Bank for International Settlement.

[2] *Op. cit.* Seventh Annual Report, p. 41, and Eighth Annual Report, p. 43.

$2\frac{1}{4}$ billion. Actually the average dollar value of new output outside the United States and the U.S.S.R. in the six years 1946–51 was $730 million, and of this $359 million went into hoards outside the United States, leaving $371 million [1] available for monetary use. Thus, had the value of gold output been sustained, the rest of the world would have obtained for monetary use nearly $2 billion worth more newly mined gold than it has actually been getting. This it could have used partly to give the United States her fair share and partly to replenish its own reserves. If new gold of this value were becoming available, it would make a big difference.

We have seen that the U.S. surplus against the rest of the world on goods and services account, excluding military end items, has been running around $2 billion a year. It would certainly not be desirable for the free world outside the United States to hand over such a large fraction ($2 billion out of $2\frac{1}{4}$ billion) of its newly mined gold each year to the United States. But if it could hand over a reasonable proportion, this would clearly make a very big contribution to paying for the U.S. surplus on current account.

The main reason for the changed gold position is that the dollar price of gold has remained fixed while the dollar price level of goods in general has considerably more than doubled. This has discouraged gold production. It has also joined with other forces to increase gold hoarding (cf. p. 69 above).

There are two aspects of this change in the position of gold which must be kept entirely separate. First there is the question of what is desirable, whether in the interests of the United States or of the world generally. Secondly there is the question of diagnosis; even if we think it quite undesirable and unnecessary to bring gold back into the picture, it makes a difference

[1] Bank of International Settlement, Twenty-second Annual Report, pp. 159-60.

to our notions of what is likely to happen or what ought to be done if we bear in mind this leading reason why the international balance is not what it was before the war. We must take the two points in order.

There is no doubt that the fixity of the dollar price of gold has gone far to reduce the part played by gold as a medium of international settlement. We may ask the question, whither the dollar? Is the future of the dollar to be that of the leading currency interchangeable with gold, as sterling was before 1914? Or is the rôle of gold now to be played down? And do the Americans desire to see the dollar established as a world paper currency in its own right, with gold purchases by the authorities being little more than a ritual and relic of times past? These are two different lines of approach, and American opinion does not appear to have made up its mind. Any reference to a revision of the price of gold is unpopular there, for reasons that will shortly be considered. This contrasts somewhat with the apparent tendency during the war period for the Americans to lay more stress than others on ideas associated with the gold standard. Indeed some British feared that the Americans desired to revive some of the less desirable features of a rigidly working gold standard. This may have been a false interpretation.

The present situation is undoubtedly awkward and anomalous. Gold can hardly resume its traditional rôle as the main medium of reserve and settlement, if the value of annual accessions continues to be so small by comparison with the growth in world trade. Gold will play a dwindling part and some other medium of international liquidity will have to be devised. This gives a problem for the future; it is not disconnected with what the Americans want to do with the dollar. We have already noted the important fact that the dollar is no longer gold-convertible for individuals. There is no doubt that, for its own convenience, the rest of the

world would like to value gold at a higher level, so that
the value of gold accessions might be raised to a more
reasonable relation to the value of increases in world
trade, against which gold has to be held as a medium
of reserve. But in the present situation the outer world
cannot raise the value of gold without thereby devaluing
their currencies against the dollar, and that, for reasons
already stated, would be most undesirable at this juncture. Thus in the existing situation, the United States
has the whip hand. If she chose to raise the dollar price
of gold — and preferably make the dollar convertible at
the same time — the rest of the world would be de-
lighted; but if she does not choose to do so, the rest
of the world has to acquiesce.

We have already seen that the great intake of gold
which occurred during the First World War and the
subsequent quinquennium, and was reinforced by another great intake owing to the flight of capital in the
'thirties, has made it possible for the United States to
have internal inflations or deflations without regard to her
gold reserves. In the period from 1939 to 1948 she allowed
a vast internal inflation to take place, and the dollar
lost about half its commodity value; simultaneously,
and by consequence, an ounce of gold lost about half
its value. The commodity value of gold depends entirely on what happens in the United States, and the
rest of the world has to acquiesce. The United States
is under no pressure to make any revision. This is
the joint effect of the large proportionate size of her
gold holding and her persistently favourable external
balance. Had these two causes not been operating, the
United States would have been under pressure to match
the debasement of the dollar in goods value by a more
or less equivalent debasement in her gold value. Even
apart from this, had the dollar been gold convertible for
individuals, the United States would have been under
some pressure to alter the dollar price. By keeping

the dollar price fixed, she has lowered the goods value of the international medium of settlement to about half, and she did not have to ask 'the world' whether this change was acceptable to it or not.

It may be desirable to take a brief glance at the reasons why some American opinion is hostile to a restoration of the value of gold. It is sometimes argued that this would cause inflation in the United States. All would grant that the marking up of existing stocks would have no such effect. But if the change of price caused a bigger annual inflow, this would set a problem for the Federal Reserve System. Assuming that under existing conditions it is providing the nation with exactly the right amount of money supply, it would have to offset the additional inflow of gold by the release of a corresponding value of securities. We have seen the importance of the accord reached with the U.S. Treasury in March 1951 concerning the maintenance of an orderly bond market. While the Federal Reserve System has gained freedom of action, it would be embarrassing to be placed in circumstances which required an inordinately large sale of U.S. Government securities. The accord might be followed by renewed discord. This is an important point; but it does not seem so important as the question whether the world is to continue to enjoy the advantages of gold as a principal medium for international settlement. It should be possible, given good will on both sides, to adjust the differences of view in regard to the bond market. If this can be done, the argument about internal inflation becomes null and void.

The second principal argument used by Americans is that, since they allegedly have already sufficient gold in Fort Knox, to mark up the gold price would be merely a way of giving the rest of the world 'aid' in a new form. But we are all trying to get away from the system of aid. Now from the point of view of the rest of the world, the purchase of more gold would not be 'aid' in the ordinary sense, since the new gold has to be produced by means of labour and other resources; this is a service for which the gold producers have to be paid; to the extent that the proximate remitters of gold to the United States were the countries of Europe, they in turn would have to buy it from the gold producers by sending out goods produced from their own factories with their own labour. No one would be getting something for nothing, as they do with 'aid' in the strict sense. All the same, a rise in the price of gold might be regarded as aid in a more subtle sense, to the extent that the Americans would be offering to pay to get more of something that they do not really need.

About this one point must be made. It would be rash to suggest that the balance of trade or the flow of international investment might some day so alter its pattern as to make the United States feel the need of a central reserve more acutely. It may be that she will continue for a long time to have a surplus on capital and current account together, and to that extent be indifferent to the size of her gold reserve. But there is one purpose of a reserve which must also be mentioned. It is a defence weapon. Unhappily, we cannot yet foresee the time in which we shall all be quite indifferent to defence potential. At $22 billion the U.S. external reserve must be regarded as miserably inadequate; it is quite out of line with all the other great defence preparations that she now has underway. Americans may be deceived by the special circumstances of the First and Second World Wars, in which the United States did not happen to be involved in the initial phase. The pattern of events would be totally different if she was involved from the outset. In an all-out effort she would not be willing to maintain a peace-time level of exports; she would have to continue to draw imports of materials from abroad; she would wish to import certain commodities not perhaps strictly necessary; in her worst hour, Britain felt that an excessive cut in the tobacco supply would be bad for morale; the Americans might feel the same about coffee; they might be under the necessity of making large disbursements abroad for the servicing of their fighting forces. Britain, a comparatively small power, and waging war on a much smaller scale than would the United States in the circumstances envisaged, overspent externally some $50 billion in the Second World War. Revaluing approximately for the change in the purchasing power of the dollar since the time when the money was spent, this may mean about $90 billion now. There is only about $22 billion worth of gold in Fort Knox. It is, of course, true that the United States might be in good credit with neutrals and could set up blocked dollar accounts in one place and another. But this is not leading from strength. It is not comfortable to depend on the varying willingness of neutrals to give credit for the financing of vital operations overseas.

The United States is running a substantial surplus on her visible trade account; she may be willing in due course to rectify the balance by buying more of various commodities; to the extent that she does not do so, she will have to face a considerable curtailment of her exports which, although not to her a fatal evil, might necessitate tiresome adjustments of employment, especially if her internal economy were not then in strong boom, as at present. It is for consideration whether it would not be quite a good thing for her to maintain some part of her present surplus in order to replenish her reserve of external assets, which, if we may judge from the experience of previous wars, would at their present level prove woefully inadequate to her needs.

We must now turn to the second aspect of the gold question. Let us suppose that no attempt is made to restore even partially the pre-war position of gold. How should recognition that the dollar gap has been caused in such large part by the change in the position of gold affect one's ideas about appropriate remedies for it? Remedy for an evil depends partly on the diagnosis of its cause.

Clearly an imbalance can only be rectified by an increase of world exports to the United States or a diminution of world imports from it.

On the one hand, the world may be able to find other goods to take the place of the gold previously remitted. Exploring possibilities on this side, we are driven to observe the protectionism of the United States. This is now of old standing. It would perhaps be unreasonable to expect a large change of attitude to take place, not in response to new claims of self-interest, but as a convenient method of helping the world to balance its account. The United States will continue to have a growing volume of imports of materials or foods that she is not well placed to produce herself. These may be regarded as essential imports. It might be possible to discriminate roughly, although not with any precision, between the imports of a nation which it would be impracticable for her to contemplate producing for herself, and those goods which are obtainable more cheaply from abroad, but can perfectly well be produced at home. There is, so to speak, the necessary importation — although nothing is absolutely necessary — and the merely beneficial importation. Where the latter would, in the absence of protection, tend to be a large part of the whole, the forces of protectionism may be expected to be strong. Britain in her heyday was in the opposite position. It must be added that there was a tremendous ideological impetus behind the inauguration of Free Trade in Britain; there was the deep thought of the great economists and the matchless oratory of Cobden and Bright, and economic argument was blended with a wider political urge in favour of the unrestricted liberty of the individual. Thus it happened that Free Trade became a highly popular doctrine in Britain, although in general Free Trade, however wise and enlightened, is not in essence a popular idea. It must remain doubtful whether there will be a grand revolt in the United States in the few years immediately ahead against protectionism. In its absence the importation of the United States may none the less be expected to grow by gradual stages. The well-known Paley Report has held out hopes that there may be a rather substantial growth within a quarter of a century.[1] But these prognostications lie beyond the period with which present policy is concerned. It is accordingly probable that the present large imbalance will have to be corrected mainly by a reduction of United States exports.

These exports have already been curtailed by discriminatory restrictions. As aid tails off, the restrictions may have to become more severe. In discussing the International Monetary Fund, we have suggested that the multilateral ideal requires in such a situation a more or less uniform intensity of restriction all round, whether or not each restricting country happens itself to be in deficit with the scarce currency country. In practice we are more likely to get a lop-sided set of discriminatory restrictions, those countries which are in normal bilateral deficit doing the major part of the work and getting a bilateral balance by means of restriction. This is clearly unsatisfactory. The chronically and normally deficit countries are those of Europe, the world deficit against the United States being not much greater than the bilateral European deficit, whether we reckon it before the war or in the last three years.

How should we wish and expect the pattern gradually to adjust itself? It would not be natural for the trade between Europe and the United States to move to

[1] *Resources for Freedom*, vol. i: *Foundations for Growth and Security* (Washington).

a bilateral balance. European exports to the United States have continued greatly to increase since the war, but, failing a sudden and far-reaching departure from protectionist policy by the United States, they are not likely to soar up to a level necessary for bilateral balance. In the last two years the exports of O.E.E.C. countries to the United States have been not far short of $2 billion a year compared with $600 million before the war. Changes both in the trading and in the invisible accounts have been so large from year to year recently that it is difficult to give any approximate figure for what might be called the present-day European deficit on bilateral account with the United States. Furthermore, the situation is perplexed by the fact that Europe has on the one hand maintained discriminatory restrictions, thus improving her balance, and on the other been encouraged by Marshall Aid and Defence Aid to make a certain number of purchases in the United States that might not have been made in the normal course of commerce. In 1951 the bilateral balance of the O.E.E.C. countries with the United States showed a deficit of approximately $2 billion; in 1952 it was only about $1 billion. 1951 may have been an abnormally bad year, both on account of the post-Korean boom and because the bilateral account on shipping was particularly unfavourable. The balance in 1952, on the other hand, was favourably affected by a considerable intensification of the restrictions. It may well be that in a normal year, even without restrictions, the deficit would not be as great as $2 billion; but it might be not very much less. Thus to get the bilateral account even by expanding exports, Europe would have to raise these to nearly double their present value; as presumably such doubling could not take place without large price concessions, the increase in volume might have to be three or four times or more. All this is clearly beyond the realm of practicality. It would also be an absurd way of trying to achieve a balance.

The natural way for Europe to balance her account with the United States is to earn dollars in multilateral exchange. It is sometimes supposed that she did this before the war, when she had a large bilateral deficit. A few dollars may have been so earned, but there was no need to earn any, since the newly mined gold was sufficient to finance the bilateral deficit several times over. Europe had, of course, to earn that gold before the war by having surpluses in third-party countries. Why is it not equally easy for her to earn the requisite dollars now ?

Before answering this, we must make a brief digression. Quite apart from the gold question and quite apart from the dollar question, Europe has had to achieve a vast increase in the volume of her exports to offset her loss of invisible income from abroad and her worsened terms of foreign trade. I have calculated that for Britain this has meant exporting annually some $3 billion worth more goods merely to buy the same quantity of imports that were bought before the war,[1] and that this constitutes some 8 per cent. of her national income and a much larger proportion of her industrial capacity. This great extra effort was required merely to enable her to buy as many imports as before the war. But she has needed a considerably greater quantity of imports to provide the raw materials of a much higher industrial output. Similar, albeit somewhat smaller, burdens have been imposed on other European countries.

First and foremost, Europe had to generate a huge increase of exports in order to pay her way; secondly, she has had to reorient them. It was not too hard for Europe to win gold by export surpluses in third-party countries because the gold was largely obtainable from the sterling area. In order to win an equivalent value

[1] Cf. Foreign Affairs, October 1953.

of dollars, it will probably be necessary to divert attention to third-party markets in the Western Hemisphere. It is no use trying to win dollars in large quantity — and a sum such as $1½ billion a year is a large quantity — in third-party markets that have not themselves a handsome dollar income. In the three years from 1950 to 1952, the U.S. dollar income on trade account of the whole world outside Europe and the Western Hemisphere was $3270 million per annum; at the same time the U.S. dollar income on trade account of Canada and Latin America was $5440 million. Still more striking is the *change* that has occurred since the pre-war period. The U.S. dollar income on trade account of the whole world other than Europe and the Western Hemisphere was, in 1950–52, about three times as great as in 1938; the U.S. dollar income on trade account of Canada and Latin America was about six times as great. It is clear, therefore, that it is in the Western Hemisphere that there is a supply of new U.S. dollars available for capture. Indeed if the countries of Europe had been on their toes immediately after the war with competitive articles available for prompt delivery to the Western Hemisphere, and if the countries there had in consequence divided their additional U.S. dollar income in reasonable proportions between purchases from the United States and purchases from Europe, the dollar would not have become a chronically scarce currency. But the Europeans were at this time heavily encumbered with their primary tasks of reconstruction and with enlarging the over-all volume of their exports and, although sales to the Western Hemisphere rose, they did not rise in an unusual proportion, and the Americans were able to come in and establish themselves in these markets. This gives point to the doctrine which I expounded forcefully at that time that the countries of Europe should have given priority to capturing foreign markets quickly and have postponed devoting resources to their own internal capital reconstruction, however desirable the latter might be. Europe has meanwhile built up her productive capacity, but how is she going to get into those Western Hemisphere markets for which she failed to compete with sufficient alacrity as they developed after the war?

There are now great difficulties. Buyers in the Western Hemisphere often appear shy of relying on European sources of supply for fear of a third World War and a renewed interruption of the channels of trade. Furthermore, strong customer relations have been established with the United States. Some American capital has flowed into those regions, and this assists trade. There is a good deal of intangible prestige and influence. Some Latin-American countries have been overspending on over-all account, and, despite the great increase of their dollar income, have overspent in dollars. They are thus at some distance from being able to supply dollars to European countries to pay for any surpluses that the latter may develop with them.

Apart from all the matters that have been mentioned there is a further obstacle to Europe obtaining dollars in third-party markets, whether in the Western Hemisphere or elsewhere, by establishing surpluses with those markets. The European currencies are soft while the dollar is hard, and it seems, and usually is, bad business to part with hard currency in payment of a soft-currency debt. It may be argued that if and when the European countries succeed in maintaining running surpluses with third-party countries, their currencies will become as hard as the dollar in those countries. But a currency is not judged only by its ephemeral or regional condition. It is doubtful whether the European currencies can be considered hard until they are convertible into the dollar.

And so we come round by a circle to the old problem of convertibility, the need for which was so much emphasized in the post-war discussions of the future of multilateral trade. Before the war, most currencies of the world were either convertible or freely marketable in foreign exchange markets, so that they had a certain equality of standing, and a nation acquiring one knew that it could get any other that it needed in exchange. Since the war each currency has been considered separately. The need of Europe is to win dollars in multilateral exchange; it is doubtful if she will be able to do so in sufficient quantity unless she can somehow restore the unity of currencies. If the European currencies were convertible, then third-party countries would part with dollars by the ordinary processes of arbitrage, scarcely knowing that they were doing so.

Thus we appear to be on the horns of a dilemma. Europe cannot make her currencies convertible, so long as she does not balance her dollar account either by direct or multilateral trade. She is never likely to earn enough dollars by direct trade, and she is unlikely to earn enough on multilateral account either unless her own currencies are dollar convertible. This appears to be an impasse. But there may be a way out of the difficulty. Europe could make her currencies convertible in the first instance, not by the healthy and natural way of earning more dollars bilaterally or multilaterally, but by intensifying her discriminatory restrictions so that she was for the time being in equal bilateral account. Britain could assist in this process by bringing home a certain quantity of dollars from the outer sterling area. If Europe could by stringent parsimony get for a time into bilateral balance with the dollar, she would be in a position to make her currencies dollar convertible and then have a much better hope of earning dollars multilaterally. On this showing, the right policy would appear to be to clamp down so drastically on dollar imports as to achieve a bilateral balance, then to hope gradually to build up a larger dollar earning from

But need to mop up surplus $ too

third-party countries and, as and when that happened, gradually to relax the discriminatory restrictions hoping one day to be able to do away with them altogether.

Some Americans regard discriminatory restrictions and inconvertibilities as merely symptoms of the same evil. They are against both, but they do not condemn inconvertibility more than discrimination; probably their tendency is the other way round, owing to the deep State Department hostility to discrimination with its long roots in history that have already been discussed. None the less it may be that the right way to obtain convertibility and non-discrimination in the long run is to aim at convertibility now at the expense of an increase in discrimination. That may be the only way of escaping from a position which appears to be becoming a stalemate.

In the foregoing paragraphs I have spoken of Europe as though she were one country. In this connection Europe is one in the sense that her countries have a common problem, namely a strong, natural and permanent direct trading deficit with the United States. The solution along the lines previously indicated could only be achieved if the European countries were prepared to act together. This does not mean that they must all make their currencies convertible at the same time, but that each must refrain from exploiting the convertibility of one or more of its European neighbours. It is outside Europe that the European countries must seek to earn dollars in third-party markets. It would be wrong for Britain to seek to earn a steady dollar income from other European countries; she might indeed contribute something to the other countries in so far as she was assisted by the whole sterling area acting together. If any one country in Europe established dollar convertibility, she would be in danger of being battened on by the others, who would take measures to establish favourable balances of trade with the convertible country, in order to get dollars out of her. The countries of Europe should strive to earn dollars in third-party countries outside Europe, but should not hope normally to earn dollars from one another, since they are all in the same boat in being in natural dollar deficit. To put this in another way, the countries of Europe should make their currencies hard to the third-party world, but should keep them soft to one another. This aim could be achieved by a further development of the European Payments Union along its present lines. Let the countries of Europe settle with outside countries on the basis of 100 per cent. convertibility and settle with each other through the machinery of the European Payments Union, which could be adapted to prevent their exploiting the convertibility of the currencies of one or more of their members. But to establish this hardness *vis-à-vis* the outer world, Europe would have to impose severer discriminatory restrictions on dollar imports than she has at present. It is to be noted that Britain has, for some years, restricted dollar imports more strongly than the continental countries; it might suffice if they raised the intensity of their restrictions to her level.

I have been led on into talking about the world-wide disequilibrium of payments. We have to recognize that this belongs essentially to the history of the dollar. Since the war the United States dollar has been differentiated from other currencies by its quality of scarcity, and dollar goods have been subjected to discriminatory restrictions. The dollar gap has been much smaller in the last three years than it was in the post-war quinquennium. Despite this, discriminations may have to be increased in future, as an offset to the reduction and eventual elimination of special American 'aid'. Are these phenomena of scarcity and discrimination likely to prove transient, or should we expect them to continue during the next two decades? It is not likely that the problem will be solved by a sufficient expansion of U.S. commodity imports, although the Paley Report raises hopes for a more distant future. It would be largely solved if the United States became willing once more to accept gold at a dollar price comparable with other post-war dollar prices. Failing that, a balance will have to be achieved by the curtailment of dollar exports.

The natural and proper way for that to come about would be by Europe taking over parts of the markets that American exporters now enjoy in other Western Hemisphere countries. Unfortunately, Europe missed the post-war bus to those parts and the Americans have become entrenched in good-customer relationships. There are also political difficulties. Europe could likewise seek to win dollars in other third-party markets, but those are not so rich in dollars.

The balance may also be redressed to the extent that third-party countries are able to supply larger quantities of commodities, such as cotton, that Europe now obtains from the United States.

To the extent that these developments do not come to pass, or only do so very gradually, there is no alternative but for that curtailment of U.S. exports which is required by the laws of arithmetic to be encompassed by still more intense discriminatory restrictions in Europe. That will not only involve a further departure from the aims expressed by Americans and British alike during the war, but will maintain a pattern of trade that is detrimental to world welfare, and not least to that of Europe. It is a case where an inferior solution has to be accepted for the time being.

A better solution could be achieved if the International Monetary Fund would bring the scarce currency clause into operation — waiving the obnoxious section already mentioned — and authorize world-wide discrimination against dollar goods. Instead of the whole burden of getting the world imbalance right being thrown on to those countries, notably those of Europe, that are in normal permanent dollar deficit, all countries, including those tending to a normal dollar surplus, would do their fair share ; there would be gentle discriminations all round instead of violent discriminations in certain regions only. This would tend to direct trade more quickly towards that new pattern which it should eventually — but tardily — assume under the forces of competition.

It is time to bring this story to a close. On the internal side, dollar prospects are fair. After a stormy history, the dollar came under the supervision of the Federal Reserve System which has succeeded in maintaining good order on the whole. The boat was terribly rocked by the great world slump. This was a phenomenon of modern capitalism and it remains doubtful if it could have been prevented by banking management alone ; it is to be hoped that new knowledge will avail to prevent any other such slump. The boat was rocked again by the Second World War, as well it might be. This was followed by an interlude in which the Federal Reserve System was left with too little power, and the needs of an orderly bond market seemed to be sovereign. The Federal Reserve System has shown that it can use its powers wisely, and the greater the powers it has, whether in the bill and bond markets, or in its power to determine legal reserve requirements, or in its power to regulate brokers' margins, or through Regulations W and X, the fairer will dollar prospects be.

Externally also the position may seem to be thoroughly satisfactory from the American point of view, since the dollar has been persistently hard to the point of scarcity. But here there are certain snags. The dollar has been too hard. Americans wish, both for reasons of age-old policies of self-interest, and also by a growing sense of responsibility for world leadership, that the dollar shall mix easily and freely with the other currencies of the world in a system of open multi-lateral trading. They aim at international co-operation on the basis of mutual understanding and friendly relations.

Something still has to be done for the full achievement of these aims. There is still thinking to be done about first principles in relation to that problem which began to manifest itself in the period 1920–24 as to how to reconcile Federal Reserve credit management designed to give a steady monetary condition inside the country with credit management designed to maintain the external account in even balance. We shall certainly not condemn credit management to maintain steady internal conditions, but we still do not see exactly how that fits in with the maintenance of an even external balance.

Then there is the question whether Americans desire the dollar to be a gold standard currency in the proper sense and wish gold to play its ancient rôle as a medium of international settlement. It was not by their wish, but by a series of accidents, that silver was displaced three-quarters of a century ago and the world put into the stricter strait-jacket of gold. Had silver still been serving as an aid to gold in a fully bimetallic system in the 'twenties, it might have made a big difference. For it was the narrowness of the gold base that caused the world, or most of it, to flee to systems of pure paper money. The rule of gold was too strict and led to a rebellion. Bimetallism with its gentler discipline might have succeeded in maintaining its sway.

If the displacement of silver impaired the power of gold to give good service as a medium of reserve and settlement, the recent degradation of the commodity value of gold itself has done no less harm. If gold is to continue to play an important part at all, the system must be loosened up. Its dollar price should be doubled.

For the rest I believe that a certain dis-entanglement of issues is desirable. These lectures have been concerned with the dollar. The dollar is a currency. In the old days the currencies of different countries were linked together by the bimetallic system, or by the gold standard, or by free markets, so that in effect the whole world had one currency. It is desirable to re-establish that state of affairs. The dollar would have an even greater part to play in such a world than she has in a world of divided currencies.

It should be the primary aim of the monetary authorities in each and every country, including the United States, and of the International Monetary Fund, to re-establish a single world currency; this implies mutual convertibility. It is quite possible to have a world currency despite an imbalance in the structure of trade and services; nay more, it is just when there is such an imbalance that a single world money may perform its most useful function. A general freedom of payments must surely ease adjustments and tend to shift trade towards a more balanced pattern.

But a doctrine has arisen recently that there is not much point in a country seeking to re-establish convertibility unless it can simultaneously discard discriminatory import restrictions. Thus convertibility is to follow in the wake of the re-establishment of trade equilibrium instead of being a prime agency for bringing that equilibrium about. Such a doctrine should be anathema to all monetary experts, and would be now, but for a certain decline in the status, authority and clear thinking of those concerned with monetary matters. If an increase of discrimination, however undesirable that may be *per se*, can achieve a unification of world currencies, the monetary authorities should welcome such an increase; they have greater fish to fry; a world money can do far more good to all the countries than discrimination can ever do harm. If the

United States authorities would relax their attitude in regard to discrimination, that might go far towards encouraging monetary authorities elsewhere to brace themselves for the task of re-establishing convertibility. From that much else would flow.

In all that I have been saying, which has contained some notes of criticism, I have never been unmindful, and we British must at no time be unmindful, of the extraordinary generosity and still greater patience displayed by the Americans in this troubled period. The rest of the world has continued to give them many good grounds for grievance, and their high and altruistic hopes have suffered repeated frustration. I am convinced that this generosity and this patience, together with a readiness to assimilate new facts and arguments, qualify them for a leadership that will stand us all in good stead in the coming years.

THE END